Obentoo 3 Workbook

おべんとう

Anne Fisher
Ayako Fukunaga
Jacqueline Brown

PINETREE SECONDARY SCHOOL
3000 PINEWOOD AVENUE, COQ. V3B 7Y7

Name	Div.	Year
James Lam	34	2006-07
Cherry Fan	61/49	2010 / 11
Ray Wang	44	2011/12
Ryah Lee	38	2011/12
kevinzhang	60	2012/2013

NELSON
THOMSON LEARNING

Australia · Canada · Mexico · Singapore · Spain · United Kingdom · United States

818

NELSON
THOMSON LEARNING

102 Dodds Street
South Melbourne Victoria 3205

Email nelson@nelson.com.au
Website http://www.nelson.com.au

Distributed in the United States and its territories by Cheng & Tsui Company Inc., Boston
Distributed in Canada by Nelson Canada
Distributed in the United Kingdom by Nelson Thomes

First published in 2001
Reprinted 2003
10 9 8 7 6 5 4 3
08 07 06 05 04 03

Copyright © 2001 Nelson, a division of Thomson Learning.
Thomson Learning is a trademark used herein under license.

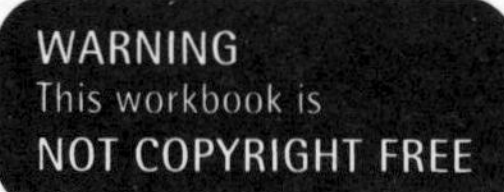
WARNING
This workbook is
NOT COPYRIGHT FREE

COPYRIGHT
Apart from fair dealing for the purposes of study, research, criticism or review, or as permitted under Part VB of the Copyright Act, no part of this book may be reproduced by any process without permission. Copyright owners may take legal action against a person who infringes on their copyright through unauthorised copying. Enquiries should be directed to the publisher.

Illustrated by Kae Sato-Goodsell
Edited by Catriona McKenzie
Publishing editor Ingrid De Baets
Production by Cindy Smith
Cover photograph by Bronek Kózka
Cover designed by Judith Summerfeldt Grace
Text designed by Kae Sato-Goodsell
Typeset in Berkeley Book
Printed in Australia by McPherson's Printing Group

Nelson Australia Pty Limited ABN 14 058 280 149 (incorporated in Victoria) trading as Nelson Thomson Learning.

Contents

Introduction

The *Obentoo 3 Workbook* will help you develop confidence in listening, speaking, reading and writing the Japanese you have learned in your *Obentoo 3 Student Book*.

The content of this book assumes you are familiar with the vocabulary and patterns introduced in *Obentoo 1* and 2. You are expected to be able to read and write the kanji from *Obentoo 1* and 2. However, if there are new readings, the furigana is given the first time the word occurs. You may have noticed there are many words in kanji but we only expect you to read and write the kanji listed inside the front cover of this book.

ちゅうい who offered helpful hints in your *Obentoo 2* and 3 *Student Books* appears again together with many other symbols which are listed below.

There is an おべんとうクイズ at the end of each unit to help you review the main content of the unit and to revise for tests. As Units 4 and 8 in your Student Book are revision units, here you will find practice of the new grammar points, and each has a respective Mock Test so that you can review the previous material. The Mock Tests also guide you to study for the tests accompanying *Obentoo 3*. These tests may be used by your teacher in class or as exams.

In the 漢字(かんじ)の書(か)き方(かた) section, there is reading and writing practice and a game or puzzle to review the kanji introduced in the unit.

At the back of this book, you will find unit-by-unit Japanese-English word lists.

がんばってね！

Anne Fisher, Ayako Fukunaga and Jacqueline Brown

 refers to further vocabulary, example patterns or other information in your Student Book.

 indicates a listening task. The *ping* indicates to pause the recording. If you want extra practice, ask your teacher if you can borrow a copy of the CD.

 indicates a speaking task which will usually be pair work.

 suggests the task is completed with a partner.

 suggests you research cultural information on Japan.

 refers to a topic for discussion either with a partner, in small groups or as a class. For example, you might like to discuss similarities and differences between Japanese culture and customs and your own.

 directs you to a website to do some exploring.

 shows that the content of the task progresses in levels of difficulty. There are often several parts to these tasks.

1 日本のメディア

1

Have you ever seen a Japanese movie, television show, advertisement, magazine, or heard a Japanese song?

Yes

What was it that you saw or heard?

Where did you see/hear it?

How would you describe it to someone?

What features were similar to those in your own country?

Were there any different features? If so, explain.

No

Are you sure? *(Think about the television shows, commercials or cartoons you watch.)*

Who watches Japanese programs, reads Japanese magazines etc? Who are they designed for?

Where could you go to find some? *(You don't have to go to Japan! Think about where they might be in your own country.)*

What examples of Japanese media would you be most likely to find easily?

2

Refer to the Unit 1 漢字の書き方 on page 124 for the stroke order practice of kanji introduced in this unit. There are also reading and writing exercises and a game or puzzle using the new kanji in this section.

3

Circle the odd word out. Be prepared to justify your answer.

a	ポケモン	セーラームーン	ファミコン	スーパーマリオ
b	アニメ	えいが	まんが	ビデオ
c	ごめんなさい	かっこわるい	らんぼうな	すくない
d	新聞	新宿(じゅく)	留学生(りゅうがくせい)	新しい

4

Listen to what the students say they do and tick the correct picture. Study the pictures before you listen to the recording.

a

b

c

d

5

Follow the script of the 会話（かいわ） on pages 2–4 of your Student Book as you listen to the recording. Answer the questions in Japanese from the information given.

a 日本にどんなざっしがありますか。

b 日本の新聞はどうですか。

c 日本のざっしはどうですか。

d オーストラリアに日本のアニメがありますか。

6

Divide the adjective sentences from the sentence bank into い or な adjectives. Then count the sounds by saying the sentence aloud. For example, とおいです。と　お　い　で　す has five kana sounds. Record the sentence in the table in the appropriate box.

Adjective sentence bank

有名(ゆうめい)です。
好きです。
いいです。
すてきです。
たのしいです。
べんりです。
いやです。
安いです。
だめです。
はずかしいです。
つまらないです。
きたないです。
かっこわるいです。
はやいです。
らんぼうです。
ざんねんです。
でんとうてきです。
おもいです。
きらいです。
すくないです。

	い adjectives	な adjectives
4 kana sounds		
5 kana sounds	とおいです。	
6 kana sounds		
7 kana sounds		
8 kana sounds		

7

Change the following い adjective sentences into the past tense and then write the English meaning for the sentences you have made.

a	新しいです。	新しかったです。	*It was new.*
b	すくないです。		
c	大きいです。		
d	高いです。		
e	すばらしいです。		
f	こわいです。		
g	おかしいです。		
h	かっこわるいです。		
i	いいです。*		

*Remember how いい changes tense!

1
三

8

With a partner, read the dialogue between Masayuki and Sumiyo and in your exercise book, write a short description in Japanese summarising Sumiyo's part. Then, make up your own dialogue using this dialogue as an example.

ヒントをください。
四時半から何をしましたか。
そのテレビばんぐみはニュースでしたか。
どんなばんぐみですか。
子どもはそのばんぐみが好きですか。
えいがでしたか。
アニメでしたか。
えーと、セーラームーンでしたか。

きのうの四時半からです。
テレビを見ました。
いいえ。
有名(ゆうめい)なばんぐみです。
はい。好きです。
いいえ。
はい。
はい、セーラームーンでした。
よくできました。

単語表(たんごひょう)

ヒントをください。	Please give me a hint.
よくできました。	Well done.

9

Change the な adjective sentences into the past tense and then write the English meaning for the sentences you have made.

a	しずかです。	しずかでした。	*It was quiet.*
b	らんぼうです。		
c	有名(ゆうめい)です。		
d	へんです。		
e	好きです。		
f	きれいです。		
g	いやです。		
h	だめです。		
i	すてきです。		

10

Listen to the comments made by the students and indicate whether the statements below are true (O) or false (X).

a ☐ The new magazine was interesting.

b ☐ The movie was scary.

c ☐ The comic was boring.

d ☐ The cartoon was funny.

e ☐ The Pokemon was expensive.

11

Complete the chart to make the negative *(it isn't . . .)* and past negative *(it wasn't . . .)* tenses of these い adjectives. In the last two columns make the past negative form into a complete sentence, and give the English for the sentence you have created.

い adjectives

a	おもい	おもくない	おもくなかった	おもくなかったです。	*It wasn't heavy.*
b	あつい				
c	やさしい				
d	新しい				
e	安い				
f	すくない				
g	かっこわるい				

12

There were lots of things you could have done over the holidays, but here are some you didn't do! Complete this task with a partner. Take turns to ask the questions and to respond using the hints given (い adjective in the past negative tense plus からです). Study the example.

なぜ海(うみ)に行きませんでしたか。
Why didn't you go to the beach?
あつくなかったからです。
It's because it wasn't hot.

You have already used から *(because)* to give reasons. Here からです *(It's because)* is used to reply in the です／ます style in accordance with the question.

a なぜスキーをしませんでしたか。(It's because it wasn't cold.)

b なぜしゅくだいをしませんでしたか。(It's because it wasn't easy.)

c なぜおばあさんのビスケットを食(た)べませんでしたか。(It's because they weren't delicious.)

d なぜ家族(かぞく)とカラオケバーでうたをうたいませんでしたか。(It's because it wasn't fun.)

e なぜおじさんのプールでおよぎませんでしたか。(It's because it wasn't very big.)

13

Listen to the recording and circle the correct alternative.

a Shingo was/wasn't good at it.

b The main character was/wasn't violent.

c I enjoyed it./I didn't enjoy it.

d The library was/wasn't quiet.

14

Complete the chart showing the changes needed to make the negative *(it isn't . . .)* and past negative *(it wasn't . . .)* tenses of these な adjectives. In the last two columns give the past negative form in a complete sentence, and then its English equivalent.

な adjectives

a	有名(ゆうめい)な	有名(ゆうめい)じゃない	有名(ゆうめい)じゃなかった	有名(ゆうめい)じゃなかったです。	*S/he wasn't famous.*
b	しずかな				
c	にぎやかな				
d	らんぼうな				
e	きれいな				
f	へんな				
g	上手(じょうず)な				

15

With a partner, practise the dialogue in Japanese and then present it to the class. You might like to add further information. Ask your teacher for the criteria if your performance is to be assessed.

A: Did you go to the movies last week?

B: Yes, I went to see *(name of movie).*

A: What was it like?

B: It was no good. It was boring.

A: Really? I saw *(name of another movie).*

B: What was it like?

A: It wasn't long. It wasn't strange. It was enjoyable.

16

Read Rumi's account of her television appearance. Answer the questions in point form in English, either in your exercise book or orally.

先週の火曜日に、私の学校のバンドがバラエティーショーでえんそうしました。みんなたのしみにしていました。先生といっしょに小さいバスでテレビのスタジオに行きました。

９時	テレビのスタジオにつきました。スタジオにがっきをもって行きました。
９時半	バンドはうたを一度れんしゅうしました。きんちょうしていました。だから、うたはあんまりよくなかったです。もう一度、れんしゅうしました。すこしはずかしかったです。
１０時半	がくやに行きました。がくやはとてもきたなかったです。びっくりしました。一人ずつ、メーキャップしました。
１１時	司会者に会いました。私たちにじょうだんを言いました。とてもおかしかったです。
１１時１５分	スタジオでまちました。スタジオはとてもしずかでした。
１１時半	バラエティーショーがはじまりました。すてきでした。
１１時４７分	バンドがえんそうしました。よかったです。
１１時５０分	コマーシャル・ブレークでバンドはスタジオを出ました。
１２時半	バラエティーショーがおわりました。
１時半	バスで学校にかえりました。

来週の木曜日にテレビでこのバラエティーショーを見ることができます。たのしみです。

- the arrival time at the studio and return time
- where they went in the studio
- what they did at each location
- how long each activity took
- how the students felt about their performance
- how their practice session went
- who they met there
- when they can see the show

単語表

えんそうします	to perform
たのしみにしていました	*(I)* was looking forward to it
つきます	to arrive
がっき	*(musical)* instruments
一度　いちど	once/one time
きんちょうしています	to be tense/nervous
もう一度　もういちど	once more
がくや	dressing room
メーキャップします	to put on *(stage)* make-up
司会者　しかいしゃ	compere
じょうだんを言います	to tell a joke
はじまります	*(something)* starts
たのしみです	I'm looking forward to it

17

In Japanese describe your favourite movie or television show. Remember to write specific things in the past tense and to use a range of verbs and adjectives. Study the example below before you begin.

- the title of the movie or television program *(heading)*
  「ブラック・レイン」
- why you are talking about it *(present tense)*
  「ブラック・レイン」は私のいちばん好きなえいがです。

単語表

あたまがいい	smart *(literally: having a good head!)*
けいさつかん	police officer
かっこいい	cool *(really good)*
やくざ	Yakuza *(Japanese mafia)*

- when you saw it
  去年テレビで見ました。
- some information about one of the characters/actors/the story
  あたまがいいアメリカ人のけいさつかんが日本に行きました。そのけいさつかんはかっこよかったです。日本のやくざはらんぼうでした。
- what it was like
  えいがはすこしこわかったです。でも、おもしろかったです。

18

Read the following dialogues while you listen to them and then write the description in English.

a A: みちよさんの車はどんな車ですか。
B: みちよさんの車ははやくて、新しいです。 ____________________

b A: あのテレビのばんぐみはどんなばんぐみですか。
B: おもしろくて、すばらしいです。 ____________________

c A: あのまんがはどんなまんがですか。
B: ながくて、つまらないです。 ____________________

19

Complete the sentences by joining the い adjectives given. Study the example before you begin.

> This chocolate is sweet and delicious. （あまい／おいしい）
> このチョコレートはあまくて、おいしいです。

a This television program is long and boring. （ながい／つまらない）
このテレビばんぐみは ____________________。

b Godzilla is big and scary. （大きい／こわい）
ゴジラは ____________________。

c This children's show is cute and fun. （かわいい／おもしろい）
この子どものばんぐみは ____________________。

d Your favourite band is noisy and idiotic! （うるさい／かっこわるい）
あなたのいちばん好きなバンドは ____________________。

e The internet is fast and convenient. （はやい／べんりな）
インターネットは ____________________。

Notice the two adjectives in each sentence reinforce each other by both saying something positive, or both saying something negative.

When you join adjectives, they both don't have to be い adjectives. Just remember the rule for connecting the first adjective.

20

Read the following dialogues while you listen to them and then write each description in English.

a A: あの人はどんな人ですか。

B: らんぼうで、いやです。 ______________________

b A: あのこうえんはどんなところですか。

B: しずかで、きれいです。 ______________________

c A: エリカさんはテニスが好きですか。

B: はい、エリカさんはテニスが大好きで、とても上手(じょうず)です。 ______________________

____

21

Complete the sentences by joining the な adjectives. In each case, a な adjective comes first, and so you will need to change it to link the descriptions. Study the example before you begin.

> That song is romantic and famous. (ロマンチックな／有名(ゆうめい)な)
>
> そのうたはロマンチックで、有名(ゆうめい)です。

a This train is safe and convenient. (あんぜんな／べんりな)

この電車は ______________________。

b Narita is an international and busy airport.* (国際的(こくさいてき)な／にぎやかな)

なりたくうこうは ______________________ くうこうです。

c Kelly's room is clean and comfortable. (きれいな／かいてきな)

ケリーさんのへやは ______________________。

d Aliens in movies are usually violent and ugly. (らんぼうな／かっこわるい)

えいがの宇宙人(うちゅうじん)はたいてい ______________________。

Notice the combination of な and い adjectives in the same sentence. Don't worry, just use the rule for joining the first adjective.

*In English it would be more natural to say Narita is a busy, international airport, but this sounds strange in Japanese.

22

Ichiro has rung Eri. Listen to their telephone call to complete the chart.

What is Eri doing tonight?

What will Eri be doing before 8:30?

It involves . . .

What is Eri going to do after 8:30?
It has . . .

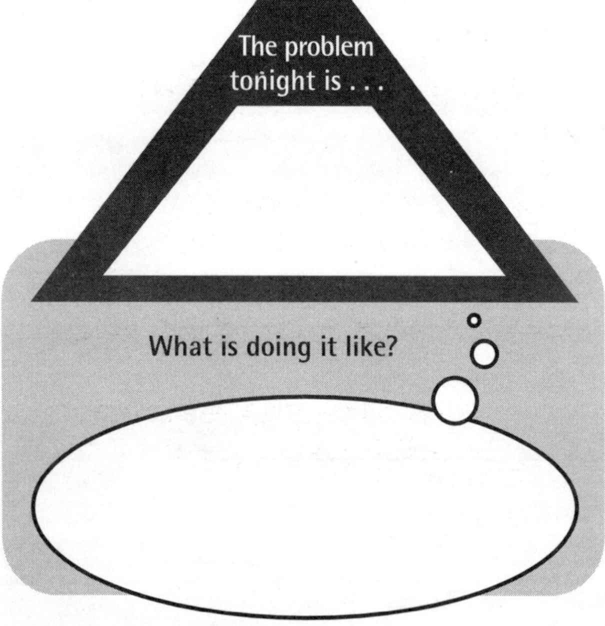

The problem tonight is . . .
What is doing it like?

What does she say about it?
What is special about tonight?

23

A Japanese exchange student, Tomoko, has brought a Japanese magazine to school. Listen to the conversation between Tomoko and Melinda. In your exercise book, in English or Japanese, note down in point form information about the following topics.

単語表（たんごひょう）

せんしゅ	player
となり	next to
出る　でる	to be published/to appear in
さいきんの	recent
じょゆう	actor *(female)*

- a) the famous singer
- b) the Tokyo Giants baseball player
- c) the model next to the baseball player
- d) the actor *(female)* on the film page

They are interrupted by a teacher. Give the English for what you think he might be saying.

24

The two sentences refer to the same item or person. In your exercise book, join the sentences as in the example and give the English for your combined sentence.

> 高村(むら)えみです。モデルです。
> 高村(むら)えみで、モデルです。
> *It's Emi Takamura and she's a model.*

a. これはプレゼントです。本です。
b. セーラームーンです。有名(ゆうめい)なまんがです。
c. コンピューターのゲームです。スーパーマリオです。
d. これはアニメです。ポケモンです。

25

Reiko, Osamu and Damien are trying to decide which video to watch tonight. Read the conversation and answer the questions in English.

おさむ：　どんなビデオがありますか。私はコメディーが大好きです。
玲子(れい)：　「ハルマゲドン」や「ビーン」や「シャル・ウィー・ダンス」や「スター・ウォーズ」、それから、いろいろなドキュメンタリーがあります。
おさむ：　ドキュメンタリーはだめですよ。
デミアン：　そうですね。「ハルマゲドン」と「スター・ウォーズ」はアクションえいがで、コメディーじゃないですね。「シャル・ウィー・ダンス」はどんなえいがですか。
おさむ：　「シャル・ウィー・ダンス」は日本のえいがで、ロマンチックな話(はなし)です。
玲子(れい)：　私は前に「シャル・ウィー・ダンス」を見ました。おもしろかったですが、また見たくないです。「ビーン」はコメディーですね。
おさむ：　「ビーン」はちょっとふるいえいがです。日本でミスタービーンはとても人気がありますよ。
玲子(れい)：　ミスタービーンはとてもおかしいです。ミスタービーンの英語(えいご)はやさしくて、分(わ)かりやすいですね。
デミアン：　ぼくもミスタービーンが大好きです。
おさむ：　じゃあ、「ビーン」にしましょう。

a. What videos are there to choose from? ______________________________

b. What do they say about:
   - Armageddon ______________________________
   - Shall We Dance? ______________________________
   - Star Wars ______________________________
   - Bean ______________________________

c. Which movie do they decide on and why? ______________________________

____

26

Part A

Keisuke wants to go to the movies with Monica, but they are having difficulties making the arrangements. Keisuke has written down his after school and weekend commitments. Listen to their telephone conversation and fill in Monica's commitments. Then suggest a time or times you think they could both go.

	けいすけ	モニカ
月曜日	テニス	
火曜日		
水曜日	ピアノ	
木曜日		
金曜日		
土曜日		
日曜日	テストのべんきょう	

何曜日に行けますか。 ______________________________

Part B

Listen to **Part B** of the conversation and compare your suggestion.

27

Join the two sentences as shown in the example and give the English.

> 毎日(まいにち)、新聞を読みます。毎日(まいにち)、テレビを見ます。
> 毎日(まいにち)、新聞を読んで、テレビを見ます。
> *I read the newspaper and watch television everyday.*

a 火曜日に、テニスのしあいをします。火曜日に、じゅうどうをれんしゅうします。

b 週末(しゅうまつ)に、えいがを見ます。週末(しゅうまつ)に、コンピューターゲームをします。

c 友(とも)だちと、買い物(もの)に行きます。友(とも)だちと、カラオケバーでうたいます。

d ふみよさんは、有名(ゆうめい)なまんがかに会(あ)いました。 ふみよさんはまんがかにインタービューしました。

28

Part A

With a partner, decide what type of group each verb belongs to and take it in turns to say its て form. Listen carefully to your partner and if you are not sure, ask her/him to write it down.

べんきょうします ⟶ べんきょうして

a うたいます　　c 食べます　　e 見ます

b 話します　　d 読みます　　f 来ます

Don't forget the different rules for each verb type.

Part B

Using the て form of the verbs in **Part A** answer these questions in Japanese. Take it in turns with your partner to question and respond. Study the example before you begin.

> 週末に、何をしますか。(study and muck around)
>
> べんきょうして、あそびます。

a パジャマ・パーティで何をしますか。 (talk and sleep)

b 図書館で何をしますか。 (read books and use the internet)

c 動物園で何をしますか。 (see lots of animals and take photos)

d 今、何をしましょうか。 (come to my house and listen to CDs)

29

Magazines often have an advice section where readers write asking for help. Read this article and decide what you think about the problem. In your exercise books, note down your ideas in English and then discuss them with a partner or the class.

単語表

日記　にっき	diary
ほかの～	another
ばんぐみ	television program
じゃまをします	to be distracting
しかります	to scold
どうしたら いいですか	What should I do?

あなたの日記

?テレビのもんだい?

Q 毎日、おとうととといっしょに学校から家にかえります。四時半にテレビで私の大好きなアニメがあります。でも、おとうとはアニメがきらいで、ほかのクイズばんぐみが好きです。おとうとはいつもテレビの前でじゃまをします。だから、テレビがぜんぜん見られません。

お母さんは、いつも私たちをしかります。私たちがうるさいからです。どうしたらいいですか。

A 月曜日と水曜日にあなたの好きなアニメを見て、火曜日と木曜日はおとうとさんが好きなばんぐみを見ます。金曜日はあなたとおとうとさんは、しゅくだいをして、お母さんがテレビを見ます。

30

Listen to 見る 聞く 分かる and answer the questions on page 11 of your Student Book. Using this information, in pairs produce a poster in Japanese for the band advertising their new album and their concert tour. Suggestions for additional information are also given.

Give the following details on your poster:

- band's name
- lead singer's name
- album's special features
- one of the songs on the album
- where the tour is going

Additional information you can make up yourself:

- album's name
- illustration of the album cover
- album release date
- tour dates
- names of the other band members
- other song titles included on the album
- any other special features

31

Refer to 見る 読む 分かる on pages 13–14 of your Student Book. In your exercise book, write a summary of Kae's day in Japanese using the information given. Use complete Japanese sentences and include details such as what she did, when, and any other relevant information.

32

With a partner, look up the movie section in a newspaper. In Japanese, discuss which movie you think is the best and why. Decide on a movie together and discuss when and where it is on. Arrange a time to see it together, how you will get there, where to meet and discuss the ticket price. Alternatively, you could use a television guide and arrange to watch a program. Discuss the details with your partner.

Try to use a variety of patterns from *Obentoo 1*, and *2* and practise the new patterns from this unit: past and negative adjective tenses, and joining adjectives, nouns and verbs.

33

Research one of the following topics about the media in Japan and identify five points of interest you can share with your class. You might like to look up the internet.

- comics (まんが／アニメ)
- newspapers (新聞)
- magazines (ざっし)

おべんとうクイズ

1 Connect the Japanese word to its English equivalent.

えいが	popular
将来(しょうらい)	a few
ファミコン	rough/violent
留学生(りゅうがくせい)	the future
五階(ごかい)	conversation
すくない	main character
人気があります	computer games
らんぼうな	animation
かしゅ	overseas exchange student
主人公(しゅじんこう)	movies
会話(かいわ)	fifth floor
アニメ	singer

2 Write the English meaning for the following words, then reproduce the stroke order for the kanji 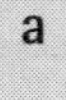 by drawing it in the air.

a 私 ______________________

b 読みます ______________________

c 聞きます ______________________

d 新しい ______________________

3 Say each of these words or phrases in Japanese and in English.

a 私のビデオ	d 聞きました
b 新しいまんが	e 読みません
c 新聞	f 見る 聞く 分(わ)かる

4 Write the て form for each verb. Check you know the meanings too!

a 見ます__________	e あります__________
b 食(た)べます__________	f 行きます__________
c 会(あ)います__________	g します__________
d 書(か)きます__________	h 話(はな)します__________

5 Say these sentences aloud in Japanese.

a	Godzilla was big.	Mickey Mouse wasn't big.
b	The magazine was cheap.	The comic wasn't cheap.
c	Jim Carey was idiotic.	Mr Bean wasn't idiotic.
d	Rambo was violent.	Forrest Gump wasn't violent.
e	The library was quiet.	The bookshop wasn't quiet.
f	Marilyn was famous.	Fred wasn't famous.

6 Read these sentences and say the meaning aloud in English.

a セーラさんは、十七才(さい)で、有名(ゆうめい)なかしゅです。

b 私のテレビは新しくて、かっこいいです。

c あのアニメの主人公(しゅじんこう)はらんぼうで、こわいです。

d 毎朝(まいあさ)、あさごはんを食(た)べて、学校(がっこう)に行きます。

7 Describe each of these pictures in one sentence giving at least two pieces of information about each one.

a

b

c

8 You are discussing videos with a friend. With a partner, how would you conduct the following conversation in Japanese?

A: I saw a movie on Tuesday. It was *Titanic* and was very interesting.
B: *Titanic*? I saw that movie. It wasn't good. It was long and boring.
A: Really? But the main characters are famous, and the music is wonderful.
B: Well, I didn't like it. I like action movies best.
A: How about coming over to my place on Saturday? *(Won't you come to my house on Saturday?)* Let's eat dinner and watch some videos.
B: OK. Let's watch *Armageddon*. The main characters are ugly and rough.
A: Hmm. Let's watch *Armageddon* and *Stuart Little*!
B: *Stuart Little*? He's small and cute, isn't he?

9 Write a review (8–12 lines of げんこうようし) on **one** of the following topics. Try to use the new patterns you have learnt in this unit. You do not need to outline the story.

- a book, comic or magazine
- a movie, animation or television show

Include the following details:

- Heading *(name of show/reading material)*
- Reviewer's name *(your name)*
- Where and when you saw/read it
- Description of the type of show/reading material including the main characters
- Your thoughts/impressions
- Recommended audience

As the action took place in the past, your description should be written in the past tense.

Look up some reviews in magazines or newspapers for reference.

10 Read the passage and answer the questions in English.

ぼくは高校一年生で、十五才です。母と父は先週、新しいコンピューターを買いました。インターネットもあります。よく家で、インターネットであそびます。いろいろなサイトがあって、おもしろいです。旅行やおんがくのサイトをよく見ます。インターネットはいろいろなことができて、べんりです。友だちにEメールもおくります。あねもよくインターネットやゲームでいっしょにあそびます。だから、母と父はあんまりつかえません。

単語表

たのしみます	to enjoy oneself
おくります	to send
あね	older sister *(your own)*
母と父　ははとちち	Mum and Dad

a Describe the writer.

____

____

b What did his parents do last week?

____

____

c What does he say you can do on the internet?

____

____

d What does he think of it?

____

____

e What does he actually do on the computer *(3 things)*?

____

____

____

f Why don't his Mum and Dad get to use the computer much?

____

____

へんな へん

1

As you know, many kanji are derived from ideographs. Match the kanji to its ideograph.

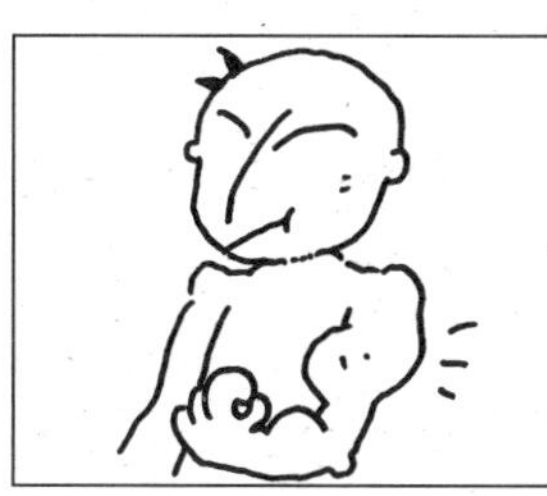

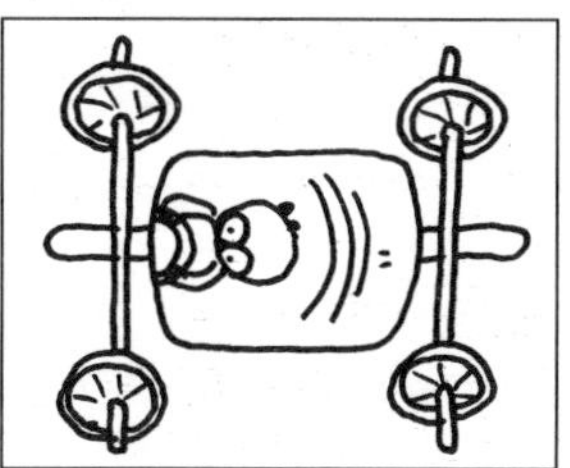

2

Find each pair of kanji which has the same radical (ぶしゅ) and then categorise them by recording them in the table below.

国	間	花	飲	使	紙
黒	雪	期	語	秋	読
電	絵	朝	見	休	回
飯	先	英	私	聞	点

へん (left side radicals)
つくり(right side radicals)
かんむり (top radicals)
あし (bottom radicals)
かまえ (surrounding radicals)

へん	つくり	かんむり	あし	かまえ

3

You will need five different coloured markers. Circle each kanji with a different colour and then find the kanji reading in each column *(right and left)*. Mark it with the respective kanji colour.

a

おん読み	かんじ	くん読み
こん	聞	よ（む）
ぶん	読	いま
どく	年	はい（る）
にゅう	今	き（く）
ねん	入	とし

b

おん読み	かんじ	くん読み
じょう	車	ちい（さい）
しゃ	小	うえ
ちゅう	中	くるま
しょう	上	まえ
ぜん	前	なか

4

Match the meaning of the kanji compounds by writing the corresponding number in the box provided.

1 up and down	2 boy	3 newspaper	4 holiday
5 summer day	6 big man	7 girl	8 adult
9 rainy weather	10 small mountain	11 half circle	12 first half

a 休日 ☐

b 男子 ☐

c 大男 ☐

d 雨天 ☐

e 前半 ☐

f 夏日 ☐

g 半円 ☐

h 女子 ☐

i 新聞 ☐

j 上下 ☐

k 小山 ☐

l 大人 ☐

5

Here is your chance to explore the interesting world of kanji by making up your own kanji name. To do this, sound out your name *(or parts of your name)* to find a kanji with a similar pronunciation. Begin with the 漢字表（かんじひょう） in the *Obentoo 3 Student Book* and if this is not sufficient, try a kanji dictionary. Study the examples before you begin.

Tobin （十瓶） （トウビン）
means *ten bottles* because he loved beer.

Ben （勉） （ベン）
means *studying* because he loved books.

Anne （安） （アン）
means *calm and soothing* because she was this kind of person.

Your English name	Your Kanji name	Meaning

2 スポーツヒーロー

1

Answer the following questions in English.

- **a** What sort of people are you attracted by or do you admire?
- **b** Is there anyone who you would like to talk to or interview?
- **c** What is sumo?
- **d** What is a traditional sport in your country?

2

Refer to the Unit 2 漢字(かんじ)の書(か)き方(かた) on page 126 for stroke order practice of the kanji introduced in this unit. There are also reading and writing exercises and a game or puzzle for you to practise the new kanji.

3

Match the answers to the questions by looking at the highlighted question words.

a	**何時に**テニスをしますか。•	•	火曜日に
b	**どこで**けんどうをしますか。•	•	学校(がっこう)で
c	**だれと**海(うみ)に行きますか。•	•	インターネットを
d	**何を**しますか。•	•	おもしろいから
e	**どのぐらい**れんしゅうしますか。•	•	友(とも)だちと
f	**おいくつ**ですか•	•	二時間ぐらい
g	**何曜日に**買い物(もの)をしますか。•	•	十六才(さい)
h	**どうして**すもうを見ますか。•	•	五時に

4

Categorise the vocabulary and phrases. (Some may appear in more than one column.)

すもう　おやつ　しあい　ばんごはん　何才(さい)ですか　どこに住んでいますか
ちゃんこなべ　お名前は何ですか　りきし　すもうべや　ひるごはん　せんしゅ

Food and eating	Sports and sumo	Interviewing phrases

5

You will be asked to listen and/or read the 会話(かいわ) in the Student Book on page 21 and then answer the following questions in Japanese.

a あゆみさんはだれにインタビューしましたか。

b ひできさんは何時から何時まで、すもうをれんしゅうしますか。

c ひできさんはごご何をしますか。

d ひできさんはあさごはんを食(た)べますか。

e ひできさんのつぎのしあいはいつですか。なぜですか。

6

Connect the ます form with its plain form.

	ます form	plain form
a	うたいます	話(はな)す
b	食(た)べます	見る
c	話(はな)します	うる
d	のります	来(く)る
e	うります	うたう
f	およぎます	する
g	見ます	食(た)べる
h	します	およぐ
i	行きます	行く
j	来(き)ます	のる

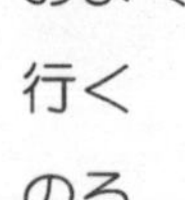

7

Complete the chart.

English	ます form	Plain form
write	書(か)きます	
die		しぬ
		あそぶ
move *(to a new address)*	ひっこします	
eat		
teach		おしえる
	買います	
ride		
understand		
return	かえります	
wait		
		およぐ
talk	話(はな)します	
go		
watch	見ます	
		うたう
		来(く)る

8

You should be familiar with how to make the plain form of verbs from the ます form verbs. Write the rules below for each group.

Group 1	Group 2	Group 3

9

Complete the verb crossword in hiragana.
All the verbs are to be written in the plain form.

たて

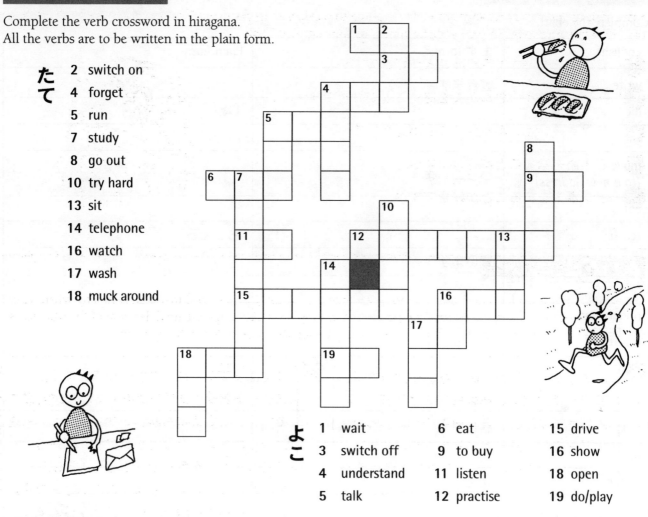

2 switch on
4 forget
5 run
7 study
8 go out
10 try hard
13 sit
14 telephone
16 watch
17 wash
18 muck around

よこ

1 wait
3 switch off
4 understand
5 talk
6 eat
9 to buy
11 listen
12 practise
15 drive
16 show
18 open
19 do/play

10

Listen to the statements and write O for 好き or X for きらい for each picture.

a

b

c

d

e

f

11

Some visiting Japanese exchange students are going to participate in your next Japanese class. They will ask you the following questions. Prepare your responses in your exercise book.

- **a** 日本語をべんきょうすることが好きですか。
- **b** ヘビーメタルのおんがくを聞くことが好きですか。
- **c** アクションえいがを見ることが好きですか。
- **d** 日本語を話すことが好きですか。
- **e** ピンポンをすることが好きですか。

12 ◎

Listen to the self-introductions from an interview conducted at the Japanese multinational company where you work. Complete the interview summary reports for each applicant. Although the final decision of the placement will be made by your boss, suggest the most suitable position/department for each applicant.

a

私の名前は山田あけみです。十六才です。高校一年生です。私は食べることが大好きです。とくに、日本のりょうりが大好きです。やきとりやすきやきはおいしいですね。でも、私はりょうりすることがきらいです。あ、トーストはつくれますよ。

b

ぼくは国高たかひろです。十五才です。スケートとサイクリングをすることが大好きです。とても気持ちがいいです。でも、あさはやくおきることはきらいです。だから、あさはやく自転車にのりません。週末に自転車にのります。およぐことも好きです。毎日、すいえいのトレーニングに行きます。

Positions vacant:

- restaurant chef
- gym instructor
- rowing coach *(morning)*
- swimming pool attendant
- sales employee in a motor bike shop
- waitress at a Japanese restaurant
- department sales manager

Name:	Name:
Age:	Age:
Likes:	Likes:
Dislikes:	Dislikes:
Suitable position:	Suitable position:

13

Your Japanese teacher has asked you to organise a fun night for next weekend. There are four options to choose from. Survey up to eight of your classmates using the 好き or きらい patterns to find the most popular activities and record their responses below.

名前	カラオケでうたう	スケートをする	えいがを見る	レストランに行く

14

Unjumble the words to make meaningful sentences and then give the English meaning.

友(とも)だち、です。、の、は、が、を、べんきょうする、大好き、日本語(ご)、クラス、こと

クラスの友(とも)だちは日本語(ご)をべんきょうすることが大好きです。

Friends in my class love to study Japanese.

a ニュース、母(はは)、の、こと、聞く、が、は、ラジオ、を、好き、です。

b です。、さむい、に、こと、きせつ、あんまり、私、およぐ、が、は、好きじゃない

c でした。、は、が、れきし、こと、父(ちち)、べんきょうする、きらい、を

d たくさんの、に、週末(まつ)、こと、です。、大きらい、しゅくだいをする、は

15

Read the passage and answer the questions in English.

私はスポーツが好きです。バレーボールをすることが大好きです。でも、サーフィンはあんまり好きじゃないです。まんがが好きで、私は本を読むことがあんまり好きじゃないです。友だちとパーティーでビデオを見ることが大好きですが、一人でテレビを見ることはあんまり好きじゃないです。

ぼくはコンピューターをつかうことが大好きです。毎日、コンピューターでべんきょうします。毎日、ピアノやキーボードもひきます。うたをつくることが好きです。ポップスのうたをひきます。サッカーやバスケットボールをすることがあんまり好きじゃないですが、ハイキングに行くことが好きです。本を読むことが大好きです。

私は、週末によく一人でリラックスします。テレビで、スポーツを見ることがきらいじゃないですが、チームスポーツをすることが大きらいです。でも、ゴルフをするのは好きです。私は、ビデオやえいがを見ることや、コンピューターゲームをすることが好きです。おんがくを聞くこともきらいじゃないです。本を読むことがとても好きです。

a Who likes to play team sports? Name the person.

(i) ______________________

b Who likes to do individual sports? Write their names and their favourite sports.

____

c Who likes to read books? Name two people.

(i) ______________________ (ii) ______________________

d Complete the chart in English.

	好きなスポーツ	きらいなスポーツ	好きなかつどう
英子			
てるゆき			
かよ			

16

Listen to the recording to find out about the speaker's abilities. Choose the correct activity and then write 上 (for 上手) or 下 (for 下手) in the appropriate square.

a

b

c

17

In your exercise book, write sentences in Japanese to match the pictures.

a

b

c

18

Read the passage and complete the table in English.

私の家族は五人家族です。父と母とあねとおばあさんです。父は四十二才です。父はゴルフが大好きです。パットがとても上手です。ハンディキャップは七です。母は、三十九才です。母はりょうりの先生です。ケーキをつくることがとても上手です。

あねは十八才です。高校三年生です。日本語をべんきょうしています。あねは日本語をべんきょうすることが大好きです。あねは日本語を話すことがとても上手です。でも、ながくて、むずかしいさくぶんを書くことがあんまり好きじゃありません。

おばあさんは六十五才です。おばあさんは、さんぽと買い物をすることが大好きです。おばあさんはセーターをつくることがとても上手です。今、おばあさんは私の新しいセーターをつくっています。

Family member	Activities s/he likes doing	Activities s/he is good at doing

19

In your exercise book, write a short piece *(about half a page)* in Japanese about your family. Include who the family members are, their ages, what they like/dislike doing and what they are good or not so good at doing.

20

Change the verbs from their potential form into the 〜ことができます pattern and then give the English meaning.

読めます	読むことができます	*I can read*
行けません	行くことができません	*I can not go*
あそべます		
話(はな)せませんでした		
うんてんできます		
来(こ)られます		
食(た)べられませんでした		
買えます		
入(はい)れません		

21

How many people in your class can do the following things? Survey your class in Japanese and record how many can or can't do each activity using the Japanese way of counting.

		できます	できません
a	おはしをつかう		
b	ケーキをつくる		
c	コンピューターで日本語を書く		
d	毎日、家で三時間べんきょうする		
e	一日に、アイスクリームを十こ食べる		
f	あるいて学校に来る		
g	コンピューターでマインスイーパーのエキスパートをする		
h	十二時間ねる		

The Japanese use the character 正 when counting groups of 5. The counting order is as follows: 一 丅 下 正 正.

22

Use the information in the pictures to complete the following sentences.

a

b

c

d

a 今晩(ばん)、パーティーに________________できません。

b レストランで大きくて、おいしい________________できます。

c 子どもの時、________________できました。

d 子どもの時、日本語(ご)で________________できませんでした。

23 ◎

Your friend is a member of an exclusive sports club. She has lent you her visitor pass for a week. Listen to the conversation about the gym timetable and some of the restrictions to answer the questions in English.

a How long is the ticket valid for?

____

b On which days of the week is the 50 metre pool available for swimming?

____

c What are the restrictions for using the gym equipment?

____

d Complete the aerobics timetable. Write the activity in Japanese.

	月	火	水	木	金	土	日
6.30–7.30	スピン						
9.30–10.30	ヨガ	サーキット	ステップ	パンプ	ステップ		サーキット
11.00–12.00			ヨガ				
5.30–6.30	ステップ			サーキット	ヨガ		
6.30–7.30	スピン	サーキット	ステップ	ヨガ			
7.30–8.30			パンプ	スピン			

24

Refer to 見る　読む　分(わ)かる on page 30 of your Student Book to complete the following information.

私の名前は、さとやたえです。

__________才(さい)です。______________年の、リレハンメル

オリンピックと______________年の長野(ながの)オリンピックに

出(で)ました。私は、________________のせんしゅです。

リレハンメルオリンピックでは１１いでしたが、長野(ながの)

オリンピックでは、____________________をとりました。

私の名前はおかざきともみです。__________________の

せんしゅです。しんちょうは__________________で、

あんまりせが高くありません。私は、1998年に、長野(ながの)

オリンピックで________________をとりました。長野(ながの)は、

東京(とうきょう)の______________にあります。長野(ながの)の町(まち)のまわりに

は、__________________がたくさんあって、

_______________にはとてもいいところです。

長野(ながの)

長野(ながの)は東京(とうきょう)の________________________ にあります。

人口(じんこう)は __________________________ で、１９９８年に、______________________

がありました。

長野(ながの)の町(まち)のまわりには、________________________ がたくさんあります。

冬はとてもさむいですから、____________________________ にはとてもいい

ところです。

2

25

Listen to 見る　聞く　分かる on page 31 of your Student Book and fill in the details in English.

名前: ______________________

しょくぎょう: ______________________

年齢: ______________________

オートバイのしゅるい *(type)*: ______________________

He started riding motor bikes: ______________________

He rode: ______________________ before motor bikes.

Why he became a cyclist: ______________________

トレーニングの時間: ______________________

好きなトレーニング: ______________________

きらいなトレーニング: ______________________

His future dreams and plans: ______________________

26

Think of one occupation and play *Celebrity Heads* in class. Students who are at the front and guessing the occupations will ask Can I . . .?, Am I good at . . .? and Do I like . . .? The other students who answer must only respond using one of the alternatives: はい、できます。いいえできません。はい、上手です。いいえ、上手じゃありません。いいえ、下手です。はい、好き・きらいです。Study the following examples before you begin the game and try to guess the occupations. Compare your responses with a partner.

a. 私は新聞を読むことが好きです。はやく話すことが上手です。それから、カメラの前で話すことも上手です。

b. 食べることと、ねることが好きです。きものをきることが上手です。ちゃんこなべをつくることも上手です。

c. 日本語を話すことが上手です。ひらがなとカタカナとかんじが書けます。生徒と話すことが好きです。

d. よくジムでトレーニングをします。車や、オートバイをうんてんすることが上手です。

27

Here is some computer terminology. Match the English to the Japanese.

a	search	チャットルーム
b	file	ウィンドウ
c	view	オープン
d	window	サーチ
e	open	ファイル
f	cancel	キャンセル
g	chatroom	ホームページ
h	homepage	ビュー
i	mail	メール

28

Here is an opportunity for you to use your Japanese skills on the Internet! Log in to a Japanese chatroom and chat with some new friends in Japanese.

Why don't you start with:

- **a** your personal profile such as name, age, origin of birth etc. (similar to a self-introduction to get to know people)
- **b** what you are good at, what you like doing (to find friends who share similar interests)
- **c** tell him/her you are looking forward to his/her reply (remember the phrases you have used in letter writing)

Do not worry if your computer can not read and write Japanese. You can still use romanisation and request a response in romanisation. Good luck in making lots of new friends!

29

It is important to know commonly used expressions and phrases by heart. The following is a sample interview between a Japanese student in Japan and an interviewer. Read the conversation and check that you understand the situation and content and then memorise it. Next, develop your own interview with a partner, using your own information *(name, age etc.)* and then perform it in class. Your teacher may assess your performance.

A: こんにちは、ちょっといいですか。
B: はい、何ですか。
A: 高校生の人の生活についてインタビューしているんですが、今、時間がありますか。
B: インタビューですか。いいですよ。
A: ありがとうございます。すみません、お名前は？
B: えんどう万里子です。
A: おいくつですか。
B: 十六才です。
A: 何年生ですか。
B: 高校一年生です。
A: そうですか。今は学校からのかえりですか。
B: はい、そうです。今日はクラブがなかったから、今から友だちと買い物に行きます。
A: 万里子さんはどんなクラブに入っていますか。
B: テニスぶに入っています。
A: いつも家にかえるのは何時ごろですか。
B: 六時ごろですね。クラブは三時間ぐらいありますから。
A: 家にかえってから、いつも何をしますか。
B: えっと、ばんごはんを食べて、友だちと電話で話します。私は電話で話すのが大好きです。毎日二時間ぐらい話すんですよ。
A: へえ、そうですか。ほかに何かしますか。
B: すこししゅくだいをします。それから、テレビを見て、まんがを読んで、私はよるはやくねることがきらいなんです。あっ、すみません、友だちがまっていますから。じゃあこれで。
A: はい、どうもありがとうございました。

30

Research a Japanese sport or sport-related topic on the Internet and make a presentation to the class. You may give your presentation orally, or on a poster or as a *Power Point* presentation.

Some topics to choose from:

- 日本のぶじゅつ（けんどう、じゅうどう、きゅうどう、からて、あいきどう）
- 日本のオリンピック
- 日本のプロやきゅう
- 日本の高校やきゅう
- 日本のJリーグ（サッカー）

おべんとうクイズ

1 Give the English meaning for the following words.

a あこがれる ______

b しあい ______

c れんしゅう ______

d きじ ______

2 Give the Japanese for the following words.

a strict, tough ______

b aged people ______

c welcome ______

d body weight ______

3 Give the kanji reading in hiragana.

a 有(ゆう)名な ______

b 今日 ______

c 上手な ______

d 来(らい)週 ______

4 Read the following sentences and circle the correct kanji combination.

a せんしゅう（先月、今週、先週）たくさんの友(とも)だちにてがみ（紙手、手話、手紙）を書(か)いた。

b けさ（毎日、今朝、今日）六時からいま（居間(いま)、今、分）まで、いま（居間(いま)、今、分）でテレビを見ています。

c まいにち（毎月、今日、毎日）おなじじかん（間時、時間、時聞）に家(うち)にかえります。

5 Write the following in kanji .

a ひとびと______ c へたな ______

b すむ ______ d ふつか______

6 Answer the following questions about yourself.

a カラオケでうたうことが好きですか。

b おはしをつかうことが上手ですか。

c ギターをひいてうたうことができますか。

d 大きくてふるい車をうんてんすることができますか。

7 Describe how to make the plain *(dictionary)* form from the ます form for each verb group.

Group 1

______

______

Group 2

______

______

Group 3

______

______

8 Change the verbs into the dictionary form.

a 見ます______

b 話(はな)します ______

c インタビューします ______

d 書(か)きます______

9 Read the sentences and choose the most appropriate alternative.

a 毎日、新聞を（読む、読みます、読んで）ことが好きです。

b 海(うみ)でながい間（およぎます、およぎ、およぐ）ことができません。

c 先(せん)週大きくて、かわいいぬいぐるみを（買います、買いました、買う）。

10 Give the Japanese for the following sentences.

a My mother is very good at playing piano.

______

______

b I like listening to the radio every morning.

______

______

c I was not good at speaking in front of people.

______

______

d I can type hiragana, katakana and kanji.

______

______

11 Give the English meanings of the following sentences.

a ジェームスくんはあつくて、ながいうどんを食(た)べることが好きです。でも、おはしをつかうことができません。

____

____

____

b みかさんは子どもの時、おんがくが大きらいでした。ピアノやギターをひくことが上手じゃなかったです。でも、カラオケでうたうことがとても上手です。

____

____

____

12 Survey a classmate in Japanese to find out the following information. Use the space below to work out your questions in Japanese.

a What sort of sports does s/he like to play?

____

____

b How long has s/he been playing the sport?

____

____

c Where and when does s/he practise?

____

____

d How many hours does s/he train everyday if s/he practises regularly?

____

____

e What does s/he hope to achieve with his/her sport in the future?

____

____

13 Read the passage and answer the questions in English in your exercise book.

私の友(とも)だちの名前は吉川(よしかわ)しんやです。十七才(さい)です。しんやくんはサッカーとやきゅうが大好きで、毎日、やきゅうをれんしゅうします。しんやくんはピッチャーで、よくホームランをうちます。でも、はやくはしることができません。しんやくんのやきゅうチームはつよかったですが、今年、トーナメントにゆうしょうすることができませんでした。

単語表(たんごひょう)

うつ	to score
ゆうしょうする	to win

a What is the name of the writer's friend?
b What does he do everyday?
c What can't he do?
d What couldn't the team do this year?

14 Read the passage and answer the questions in Japanese.

中西(にし)まさきさんは学校(がっこう)のたいいくの先生(せんせい)です。中西先生(にしせんせい)はけんどうと、サッカーとじゅうどうをすることがとても上手です。学校(がっこう)のクラブで、バレーボールもおしえています。中西(にし)先生(せんせい)はけんどうの子どもチャンピオンでした。中西先生(にしせんせい)は、スポーツをすることが大好きです。でも、スポーツを見ることはあんまり好きじゃありません。

a 中西先生(にしせんせい)はだれですか。

____

____

b 中西先生(にしせんせい)は何をすることがとても上手ですか。

____

____

c 中西先生(にしせんせい)はスポーツを見ることが大好きですか。

____

____

3 留学生 (りゅうがくせい)

1

Refer to じゅんびたいそう on page 38 in your Student Book to answer the questions in English in your exercise book.

a. List the information you have learnt about school in Japan.

b. Have you heard anything else about school life in Japan? If so, explain.

c. How does school life in Japan compare to your school life?

2

Refer to the Unit 3 漢字(かんじ)の書(か)き方(かた) on page 130 for the stroke order practice of the kanji introduced in this unit. There are also reading and writing exercises and a game or puzzle for you practise the new kanji.

3

This is a **hiragana** crossword with three types of clues. For the clues written in かんじ, transpose them into ひらがな. For the words in English, give the equivalent Japanese. For clues with gaps, complete the word. All verbs are in plain form unless otherwise stated.

よこ

2 to come
5 art
7 economics
9 to understand
12 自分の
13 gymnastics
14 a country's national language
16 neatly
17 bought (ます form)
19 lateness
21 classroom
23 to clean up
25 school rules
29 young
30 留学生(りゅうがくせい) りゅう____
31 bathroom
32 行く
33 about 5 o'clock
35 二時に

たて

1 first day
2 shoes
3 電話(でんわ)
4 student
6 make-up
8 period one
10 subject
11 新しい
14 高校
15 午前中(ごぜんちゅう)
16 rules
17 to chew
18 physical education
20 to meet
21 to wear *(clothes)*
22 to arrive
23 after that
24 maths
26 indoor shoes
27 finally
28 bath
32 今

4

You will be asked to listen and/or read the 会話(かいわ) in your Student Book on page 39 and then answer the following questions in Japanese.

a メリッサさんは学校でだれに会(あ)いましたか。

b せいふくのきそくはどんなきそくですか。

c 久子(ひさ)さんとメリッサさんは、今日、どんなかもくをべんきょうしましたか。

d トイレのげたはどこではかなければなりませんか。どこではいてはだめですか。

5

Listen to the statements about the school rules and number these pictures in the order that you hear them.

a

b

c

d

e

f

g

h

6

Change these verbs to match the English given by using the （〜な）ければなりません pattern.

	Group 1 verbs		
a	まつ	I must wait.	
b	会(あ)う	You must meet.	
c	ぬぐ	You must take off *(shoes etc).*	
	Group 2 verbs		
d	食(た)べる	I must eat.	
e	出る	I must leave.	
f	きる	You must wear it.	
	Irregular verbs		
g	そうじする	I must clean up.	
h	来(く)る	You must come.	

7

Melissa is chatting on the phone with Kurt who is an exchange student from Germany. He is at a different Japanese school to Melissa. The only language they have in common is Japanese! Listen to their conversation and either draw or note down in point form what Kurt and Melissa mention they need to wear at school. They also discuss what they wear at school in Germany and New Zealand respectively. You might like to draw or note down this information in your exercise book.

単語表(たんごひょう)

つかれる	to get tired
何もすることができません	can't do anything
一日中 いちにちじゅう	all day
ユニフォーム	*(sports)* uniform
*(noun)*の時に	when we . . .
エプロンをする	to wear an apron

8

Read Cathy's letter to her penfriend Eri and in your exercise book draw up Cathy's schedule.

えりさんへ、

こんにちは。お元気ですか。きのう、えりさんのお手紙をもらいました。どうもありがとう。

えりさんはいつも週末に何をしますか。えりさんもいそがしいでしょう。私は今週末、いろいろなことをします。私は好きな人がいます。それで、土曜日にかれのたんじょう日パーティーに行きます。

まず、金曜日に、学校のあとで、ぶかつに行かなければなりません。私はおんがくぶに入っています。来月、学校のコンサートでベースギターをひきます。だから、コンサートの前に、たくさんれんしゅうしなければなりません。

ぶかつのあとで、友だちのともみさんと買い物に行きます。デパートに行って、かれの誕生日プレゼントを買います。かっこいいセーターが買いたいです。それから、ぶんぼうぐやに行って、誕生日カードをさがします。私の新しいようふくも買います。私は買い物をすることがとても好きです。

土曜日はパーティーの前に英語のしゅくだいをしなければなりません。私はさくぶんを書くことが上手です。でも、むずかしくて、たいへんです。しゅくだいは、いやですね。でも、パーティーはたのしみです。パーティーで、ビデオを見て、友だちと話します。でも、おさけを飲んでは、だめです。今度、そのパーティーについて書きます。

ご家族のみなさんによろしく。じゃあ、また。お元気で。

五月二十三日　水曜日

マローニ・キャシーより

単語表

今度　こんど next time

〜について　about

9

Write these sentences in Japanese, using the（〜て）はだめです pattern.

a You must not chew.（かむ）

b You shouldn't go in.（入る）

c You mustn't wear make-up.（けしょうする）

d You shouldn't wear jewellery at school.（つける）

e You must not play around/muck around.（あそぶ）

10

Natalie's family is hosting a Japanese exchange student, Nanayo Iwashita. Natalie and her younger sister Trisha are learning Japanese. Trisha has decided she will tell Nanayo all the school rules she can think of, but she gets a bit carried away!

明日(あした)、私の学校でのはじめての日ですね。どんな校則(こうそく)がありますか。

校則(そく)ですか。校則(そく)はたくさんありますよ。たとえば、ガムをかんではだめです。それから、ろうかではしってはだめです。

せいふくは？

私たちの学校はせいふくがありません。だから、好きなようふくをきてもいいです。アクセサリーもつけてもいいです。でも、おけしょうをしてはだめです。

そうですか。日本とぜんぜんちがいますね。

ああ、そうですか。日本の学校ではどうですか。

ええと、好きなようふくをきてはだめです。せいふくをきなければなりません。

ほんとうですか。

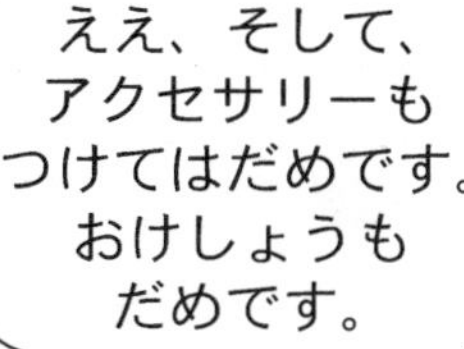

ええ、そして、アクセサリーもつけてはだめです。おけしょうもだめです。

ええ。きびしいですね。きょうしつではどうですか。私たちの学校では、じゅぎょう中にたってはだめです。でも、時々、友(とも)だちと話(はな)してもいいです。

日本では、じゅぎょう中にはもちろんたってはだめです。それから、友(とも)だちと話(はな)してはだめです。でも、先生に話(はな)してもいいです。

ええ、日本の学校はきびしいですね。

でも、おなじ校則(そく)もすこしありますね。

単語表(たんごひょう)

はしる	to run
ちがう	to differ
たつ	to stand

Complete the chart in English, listing all the rules Trisha and Nanayo mentioned. Then, place a 0 next to the rules that apply or a X next to those that don't at Trisha and Nanayo's own schools respectively.

	校則（そく）	トリーシャの学校	ななよの学校
a			
b			
c			
d			
e			
f			

11

Listen to the sets of rules and decide where they might apply. Use the Japanese word for the location/activity for as many of your answers as you can.

a ______________________

b ______________________

c ______________________

12

Listen to the information each person gives about their interests. Place a ○(まる) next to the pictures that accurately represent what has been said, and a ×(ばつ) beside those that are inappropriate.

単語表（たんごひょう）
すいそうがくぶ
brass band club

a

b

c

d

e

f

13

バスケットボールのチームに入っていますか。Follow the maze tunnels to discover which team or club each student belongs to, wants to belong to, or belonged to. Write your sentences below. Don't forget to add the appropriate particles.

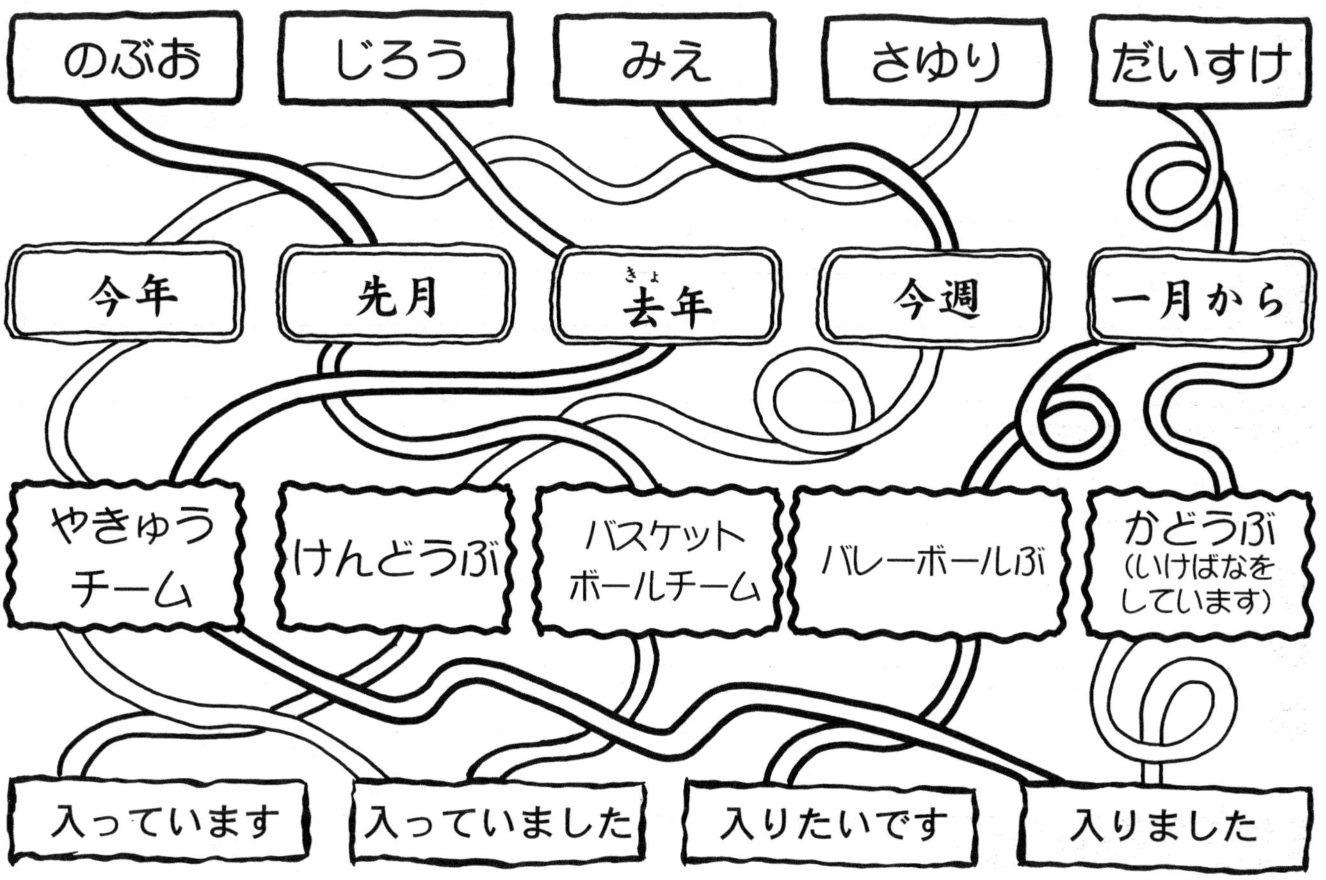

a のぶおくんは、先月バスケットボールチームに入っていました。

b じろうくんは、 ______________________________

c みえさんは、 ______________________________

d さゆりさんは、 ______________________________

e だいすけくんは、 ______________________________

14

クラブに入っていますか。List all the clubs and teams that you belong to, or have belonged to in the past. (These could become the start of your personal resume.) Choose one of the things on your list for this exercise. Working with a partner, take it in turns to ask each other the following questions about his/her choice, and respond in Japanese. Remember to use the past tense if you used to be a member of the one you have chosen.

- クラブに入っていますか。
- どんなクラブに入っていますか。
- 何年間ぐらい入っていますか。
- どうですか。

15

Read the following introduction of Rachel's family and complete the chart in Japanese showing what clubs each of her family members belong to.

はじめまして。私はレーチェルです。家族は七人です。父は四十才で、スポーツが好きです。とくに、ゴルフが上手です。ゴルフクラブに入っています。毎週土曜日にゴルフをしています。母は三十八才で、おんがくが好きです。コーラスクラブに入っています。毎週うたって、れんしゅうに行きます。あには大学一年生です。大学の新聞ぶに入っています。きじを書くことが上手です。週末に家で新聞きじを書いています。おとうとは中学三年生で、まんがをかくことが大好きです。学校のアニメぶに入っています。毎日友だちとえをかいています。上のいもうとは中学一年生です。ダンスぶに入っていて、毎週木曜日にれんしゅうしています。下のいもうとは小学五年生で、はしることが上手です。りくじょうぶに入っています。いつも学校ではしっています。私はうまが好きで、学校のじょうばぶに入っています。毎週末れんしゅうします。みんな、いそがしいです。でも、たのしい家族です。どうぞよろしくおねがいします。

単語表

コーラスクラブ	choral group
りくじょうぶ	athletics club

	どんなクラブに入っていますか	いつしますか
父		
母		
あに		
おとうと		
上のいもうと		
下のいもうと		
レーチェル		

16

In English, explain what you need to do for the following activities.

テニスのゲームの前に、テニスのユニフォームを買わなければなりません。

Before the tennis game, I must buy a tennis uniform.

a ジョギングの前に、じゅんびたいそうをしなければなりません。

____

b けんどうのしあいの前に、れいをしなければなりません。

____

c 旅行(りょこう)の前に、カメラを買わなければなりません。

____

d バンドのコンサートの前に、れんしゅうしなければなりません。

____

e コンピュータークラブの前に、フロッピーを買わなければなりません。

____

17

In pairs, practise answering the following questions saying what you do before each of the activities given. Answer in complete sentences as in the example.

あさごはんの前に、何をしますか。

あさごはんの前に、せいふくをきます。

a テニスのゲームの前に、何をしますか。

b えいがの前に、何をしますか。

c ばんごはんの前に、何をしますか。

d 数学(すうがく)のじゅぎょうの前に、何をしますか。

18

Listen to the order of the pairs of statements and write ○ if the order is correct or × if it is not, according to what you hear.

a

b

c

d

e

19

Listen to the activities which are done **before** or **after** school. Note down the order the activities occur in English.

a ______________________________

b ______________________________

c ______________________________

d ______________________________

20

> **単語表**(たんごひょう)
>
> さんぽ　a walk/stroll

Write the sequence of events for the following activities in Japanese in your exercise book, using the pattern *(activity)* のあとで.

21

Which came first? With a partner or in groups, read the sentences and work out the order of the activities from the clues given. Write the sequence of the activities in your exercise book.

- **a** ジョギングのあとで、あさごはんを食(た)べました。
- **b** アルバイトのあとで、友(とも)だちとすこし買い物(もの)をしました。
- **c** あさごはんの前に、シャワーをあびました。
- **d** じゅぎょうのあとで、ぶかつに行きました。
- **e** あさごはんのあとで、バスで学校に行きました。
- **f** アルバイトの前に、ぶかつに行きました。

22

Part A

In Japanese, fill in the chart by writing a time for each activity. Add one or two activities of your own. Then number each activity in the order that you do them.

	何時？ 私		何時？ 友だち	
あさごはん				
かつどう				
ひるごはん				
しゅくだい				
スポーツ				
テレビ				

Part B

In pairs, take it in turns to talk about the order of the things on your list by making sentences using the ～あとで pattern. Your partner will then ask you what time you did each activity and will fill in each time accordingly. Then swap roles.

Part C

After completing **Part B**, report back to your partner, in reverse order by using the ～前に pattern and the past tense to say what your partner did on that day. Study the example.

えいがの前に、ごはんを食(た)べました。

23

どんなかなを書(か)きましょうか。

Review these terms, then complete the Venn Diagram by labelling each area with one of the five terms below.

かな　general term for hiragana and katakana

かたかな　used for foreign words, names etc.
（オレンジ、メリッサ）

ひらがな　generally used for words in Japanese
（ぜんぜん、いろいろな）

ふりがな　small hiragana above kanji to show pronunciation
（新聞(しんぶん)、五時間(ごじかん)）

おくりがな　hiragana used to complete kanji words such as verbs, adjectives, etc.
（読みます）（高かかったです）

Venn Diagram

Title:

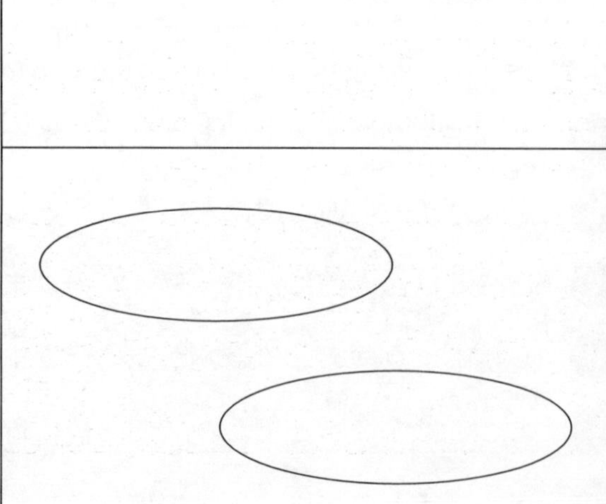

3

24

Part A

Listen to 見る 聞く 分かる on page 50 of your Student Book to fill in the order of the following topics according to the conversation between Hisako, her mother and Melissa.

a ☐ having a cup of tea

b ☐ discussing what was for dinner

c ☐ talking about the difficulties of speaking a foreign language all day

d ☐ discussing the time dinner was going to be

e ☐ greetings

f ☐ having a rest

g ☐ discussing the bath procedures

h ☐ discussing school

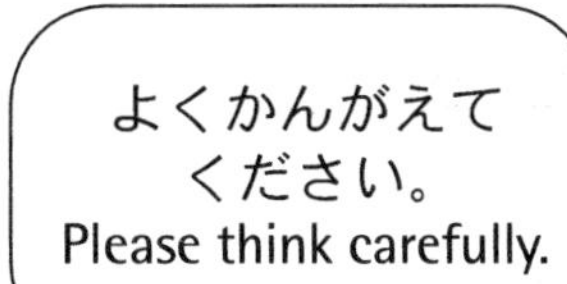

よくかんがえて
ください。
Please think carefully.

Part B

Discuss the following issues in pairs or small groups. You might like to note down your ideas.

a If you had to explain to a Japanese person how to use your bath or shower, what would you emphasise?

b How you would cope having to speak only Japanese all day? How do you think it would affect the way Japanese people relate to you?

25

Refer to 見る 読む 分かる on pages 48–9. Create a picture album to accompany Melissa's article as if it was being read out. Illustrate six to eight of the points she mentions. The captions below may help you get started. Your picture album could be drawings, photos that accurately reflect the details in the article, a *Power Point* presentation or a series of overheads.

メリッサさんの家族	さようならパーティー	ホストのおねえさん
好きなかもく	レストランで	日本の学校
あねといっしょに	ホストのお母さん	

26

Present an information package for future exchange students visiting your school.

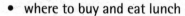

Presentation ideas:
brochure
magazine
on-screen presentation
musical presentation
web page
poster
video

Title:	name of your school (and motto if applicable)
Audience:	Japanese exchange students
Purpose:	to present an introduction to your school
Style of presentation:	informative
Organisation:	work individually or in small groups
Length:	equivalent of 1–$1\frac{1}{2}$ pages of げんこうようし per group member

Choose a selection of topics from this list. You must include the points marked * to demonstrate your understanding of the new patterns introduced in this unit.

- school location and transport
- school map
- school population and teachers
- school subjects and activities
- the number of lessons per day and home room arrangements
- where to buy and eat lunch
- what to do before and after school*
- clubs and sports teams you can join*
- some basic school rules*
- highlights of the school year

Include illustrations and visual prompts to help the exchange students understand the details of your information.

27

Over the telephone, explain the rules in your home or in the school boarding house to a fellow student. In your conversation, mention two things you may do, three things you can't do and three things you must do. Practise with a partner and see if they can work out the rules.

Here are some suggestions.

- 学校のあとで、時々買い物(もの)に行ってもいいです。
  Sometimes you may go shopping after school.
- 七時から九時までテレビを見てはだめです。
  You must not watch television from 7 to 9.
- へやをそうじしなければなりません。
  You must clean your room.

28

Research one of the following topics about Japan, and present your findings to the class. Try using the Internet.

3
四十八

おべんとうクイズ

1 Match each word with its English equivalent.

せいふく ·	· to wear *(accessories)*
そうじする ·	· young
じゅぎょう ·	· to take off *(clothes)*
わかい ·	· to clean
はく ·	· finally
それから ·	· *(school)* uniform
アクセサリー ·	· classroom
うわばき ·	· class
ぬぐ ·	· to wear *(pants etc)*
さいごに ·	· and then, and also
つける ·	· indoor shoes
きょうしつ ·	· accessories

2 Write the following kanji words in hiragana and check you know the meaning.

a 出る __________

b 学校 __________

c 留学生 りゅう __________

d 入る __________

e 高校 __________

f 家 __________

g 先生 __________

h 自分の __________

3 Complete the following sentences by adding the appropriate kanji words.

a ふじわら_____（せんせい）はきびしくないです。

b _____（らいしゅう）、_____（こうこうにねんせい）は動物園（どうぶつえん）にえんそくに_____（い）きます。

c 将来（しょうらい）、_____（じぶん）の_____（うち）を_____（か）いたいです。

d 空（から）_____（て）ぶに_____（はい）っています。

e _____（きょう）、_____（ごじはん）ごろに_____（がっこう）を_____（で）ました。

4 In your exercise book, write the English for the sentences in Question 3.

5 Give the Japanese for the following.

a 食（た）べる __________

You must: __________

You must not: __________

b おけしょうをする

You must: __________

You must not: __________

c つく

You must: __________

You must not: __________

d ぬぐ

You must: __________

You must not: __________

e かむ

You must: __________

You must not: __________

f 入れる

You must: __________

You must not: __________

g はく

You must: __________

You must not: __________

h きる *(to wear)*

You must: __________

You must not: __________

6 Make up a sentence in Japanese to say what you would do **before** each of these activities, and another to say what you do **after**.

a シャワー

b えいが

c パーティー

7 How would you tell someone you belong to these clubs or teams?

a バドミントンぶ

b けんどうぶ

c サイクリングクラブ

8 Highlight the true statements.

a たたみの上をくつであるいてはだめです。

b 学校で、ガムをかまなければなりません。

c 日本の家ではおふろの中で、かみのけをあらってはだめです。

d じゅぎょう中にあそんではだめです。

e きょうしつで、トイレのスリッパをはかなければなりません。

f 日本の高校では生徒(と)はおけしょうをしてはだめです。

9 An exchange student is talking to a student from your school. With a partner, work out the following conversation in Japanese.

E: Exchange student
S: Student from your school

E: What sort of school rules are there?
S: Well, you must wear a *(school)* uniform everyday.
E: Really? Can I wear jewellery?
S: No, you mustn't.
E: The school rules are strict aren't they?
S: Yes, they are. I belong to the school film club. Tomorrow we're going to the movies after school. Do you want to come too?
E: Yes, thanks, I'd love to. I love going to see movies.

10 Write an information card for an exchange student to help him/her on him/her first day at your school.

Task: handy information pocket-size card
Audience: exchange student's first day at your school
Style: informative
Length: 150-200 字(じ)
(a sheet of げんこうようし=400字(じ) [400 characters])

Include:

- what time school starts and finishes
- some classes
- three things they must do
- three things they must not do *(These can be school rules or handy survival hints.)*
- suggest a team or club they can join

11 Read Kooichiro's postcard and give details about the topics below based on Kooichiro's experiences. Answer in English.

おじさんへ、

お手紙(がみ)をどうもありがとうございました。先週の月曜日は、オーストラリアの高校でのはじめての日でした。あさ、学校の前に自転車(てんしゃ)で友(とも)だちのジャックくんの家に行って、いっしょにバスで学校に行きました。八時半ごろに学校につきました。高校は家からとおくないです。

校則(そく)はきびしいです。たとえば、ガムをかんではだめです。もちろん、たばこをすってはだめです。でも、女の子はおけしょうをしてもいいです。

毎週、生徒(と)はみんなスポーツをしなければなりません。ぼくはフットボールのチームに入っています。オーストラリアのフットボールはおもしろくて、人気があります。ぼくはサッカーができます。でも、まだ「オージー・ルール」のフットボールは上手じゃないです！サッカーとフットボールはルールがぜんぜんちがいます。

おへんじをおまちしています。それでは。

2003年5月19日　　　　こういちろうより

a **Getting to school:**
- When? ______
- How? ______
- Who with? ______

b **School rules:**
- How does he describe them?

______

______

- Give an example.

______

c **Sport:**
- What team has he joined?
- Why? ______
- What does he think of the game so far?

______

______

すらすら じしょけい

1

Here is a handy reference list of the plain forms of い and な adjectives.

い Adjectives

English	Present	Present negative	Past	Past negative
delicious	おいしい	おいしくない	おいしかった	おいしくなかった
noisy	うるさい	うるさくない	うるさかった	うるさくなかった
cute	かわいい	かわいくない	かわいかった	かわいくなかった
scary	こわい	こわくない	こわかった	こわくなかった
strong	つよい	つよくない	つよかった	つよくなかった
long	ながい	ながくない	ながかった	ながくなかった
good	いい	よくない	よかった	よくなかった

な Adjectives

English	Present	Present negative	Past	Past negative
safe	あんぜんだ	あんぜんじゃない	あんぜんだった	あんぜんじゃなかった
dislike	きらいだ	きらいじゃない	きらいだった	きらいじゃなかった
quiet	しずかだ	しずかじゃない	しずかだった	しずかじゃなかった
like	好きだ	好きじゃない	好きだった	好きじゃなかった
lively	にぎやかだ	にぎやかじゃない	にぎやかだった	にぎやかじゃなかった
strange	へんだ	へんじゃない	へんだった	へんじゃなかった

2

Sort the plain forms of these adjectives into their correct type (い or な) and record them in the table below. When you have finished, check your answers with a partner.

とおくない　べんりだった
だめだ　すてきじゃなかった
よくない　ひくくなかった
まずかった　すくなくない
きれいだ　やさしかった
いっぱいだ　さびしくない
あつい　じょうずじゃない
いやだ　らんぼうだった

い Adjectives	な Adjectives

3 

Refer to the Adjective Chart below and repeat what you hear. Each adjective will be given in English, then in Japanese in its polite form and then the equivalent plain form.

い Adjectives

English	Present (Polite form)	Present (Plain form)	Present negative (Polite form)	Present negative (Plain form)
light/bright	あかるいです	あかるい	あかるくないです	あかるくない
warm	あたたかいです	あたたかい	あたたかくないです	あたたかくない
new	あたらしいです	あたらしい	あたらしくないです	あたらしくない
hot/thick	あついです	あつい	あつくないです	あつくない
dangerous	あぶないです	あぶない	あぶなくないです	あぶなくない
good	いいです	いい	よくないです	よくない
busy	いそがしいです	いそがしい	いそがしくないです	いそがしくない
thin	うすいです	うすい	うすくないです	うすくない

な Adjectives

English	Present (Polite form)	Present (Plain form)	Present negative (Polite form)	Present negative (Plain form)
safe	あんぜんです	あんぜんだ	あんぜんじゃないです	あんぜんじゃない
full	いっぱいです	いっぱいだ	いっぱいじゃないです	いっぱいじゃない
unpleasant	いやです	いやだ	いやじゃないです	いやじゃない
comfortable/ pleasant	かいてきです	かいてきだ	かいてきじゃないです	かいてきじゃない
dislike	きらいです	きらいだ	きらいじゃないです	きらいじゃない
pretty/clean	きれいです	きれいだ	きれいじゃないです	きれいじゃない
international	国際的(こくさいてき)です	国際的(こくさいてき)だ	国際的(こくさいてき)じゃないです	国際的(こくさいてき)じゃない
quiet	しずかです	しずかだ	しずかじゃないです	しずかじゃない

4

Follow the Verb Chart in your Student Book on pages 162–3 and repeat what you hear. The verbs will be given in English then in Japanese in the polite (ます) form and then the equivalent plain form.

5

Listen to the verbs in the plain form and write them below. Then write the ます *(polite)* form.

a ______________________ f ______________________

b ______________________ g ______________________

c ______________________ h ______________________

d ______________________ i ______________________

e ______________________ j ______________________

Past (Polite form)	Past (Plain form)	Past negative (Polite form)	Past negative (Plain form)
あかるかったです	あかるかった	あかるくなかったです	あかるくなかった
あたたかかったです	あたたかかった	あたたかくなかったです	あたたかくなかった
あたらしかったです	あたらしかった	あたらしくなかったです	あたらしくなかった
あつかったです	あつかった	あつくなかったです	あつくなかった
あぶなかったです	あぶなかった	あぶなくなかったです	あぶなくなかった
よかったです	よかった	よくなかったです	よくなかった
いそがしかったです	いそがしかった	いそがしくなかったです	いそがしくなかった
うすかったです	うすかった	うすくなかったです	うすくなかった

Past (Polite form)	Past (Plain form)	Past negative (Polite form)	Past negative (Plain form)
あんぜんでした	あんぜんだった	あんぜんじゃなかったです	あんぜんじゃなかった
いっぱいでした	いっぱいだった	いっぱいじゃなかったです	いっぱいじゃなかった
いやでした	いやだった	いやじゃなかったです	いやじゃなかった
かいてきでした	かいてきだった	かいてきじゃなかったです	かいてきじゃなかった
きらいでした	きらいだった	きらいじゃなかったです	きらいじゃなかった
きれいでした	きれいだった	きれいじゃなかったです	きれいじゃなかった
国際的(こくさいてき)でした	国際的(こくさいてき)だった	国際的(こくさいてき)じゃなかったです	国際的(こくさいてき)じゃなかった
しずかでした	しずかだった	しずかじゃなかったです	しずかじゃなかった

Part A

Circle the correct plain form ending to match each of the polite form of the verbs given.

Group one verbs

a もらいます
- もらわない
- もらう
- もらわない

b はじまりません
- はじまらない
- はじまらなかった
- はじまった

c 書きませんでした
- 書(か)く
- 書(か)かない
- 書(か)かなかった

d 飲(の)みました
- 飲(の)まない
- 飲(の)む
- 飲(の)んだ

e たちます
- たたない
- たつ
- たった

f 聞きました
- 聞かない
- 聞く
- 聞いた

Group two verbs

g おしえます
- おしえる
- おしえない
- おしえた

h ねませんでした
- ねない
- ねた
- ねなかった

i わすれません
- わすれない
- わすれる
- わすれなかった

j すてました
- すてない
- すてた
- すてる

k 見せませんでした
- 見せなかった
- 見せない
- 見せた

l きめます
- きめない
- きめる
- きめた

Irregular verbs

m 電話します
- 電話する
- 電話しない
- 電話した

n 来ません
- 来た
- 来る
- 来ない

o でした
- だ
- じゃない
- だった

Part B

Give the English for your answers in **Part A**.

a ______________________________

c ______________________________

d ______________________________

h ______________________________

i ______________________________

l ______________________________

m ______________________________

o ______________________________

7

Read the following diary entry. In your exercise book, rewrite it in the polite form so that you can present it as a speech to your class. Add an appropriate introduction and conclusion.

七月二十三日　水曜日　はれ

先週家族といっしょに長崎に行った。とてもむしあつかった。千六百年ごろから、ポルトガル人やオランダ人などが長崎に住んでいた。西洋的な建物がたくさんある。私たちは有名なグラバーていを見物した。そのあとで、きっさてんでこうちゃを飲んで、カステラを食べた。おいしかった。長崎はとてもおもしろい町だ。

単語表

西洋的な せいようてきな	Western style
グラバーてい	Glover House
カステラ	sponge cake

4 くものいと

1  

The story in じゅんびたいそう is a typical Buddhist tale. The moral aims to help people learn to lead a better life. Answer these questions in English in your exercise book or discuss them with a partner.

- **a** What are some of the central themes in this tale?
- **b** Is there a traditional or religious story that you know with a similar moral?
- **c** If you were writing this story today, what modern setting would you use?

2

The following words are introduced in this unit and relate to Japanese religions. Match the Japanese with either the English or the pictures.

a	じんじゃ	Shinto priest
b	おてら	
c	ぶつぞう	shrine
d	つりがね	Buddhist
e	かんぬし	Buddhist temple
f	ぶっきょうと	
g	とりい	

3  

You will be asked to listen and/or read くものいと. According to this folktale circle はい or いいえ for each statement.

a	All good people go to heaven.	はい	いいえ
b	Buddha lived in heaven.	はい	いいえ
c	Kandata lived in heaven.	はい	いいえ
d	Kandata did lots of bad things when he was alive but he did not tell lies.	はい	いいえ
e	Kandata killed many spiders when he was alive.	はい	いいえ
f	There are many trials in hell.	はい	いいえ
g	In hell, Kandata saw a spider walking near the trial.	はい	いいえ
h	Kandata slowly but steadily climbed all the way up the spider thread.	はい	いいえ
i	Kandata struggled to keep climbing up the spider thread.	はい	いいえ
j	In hell, many people fought each other when climbing up the spider thread.	はい	いいえ
k	Kandata was happy when he saw many people climbing up the spider thread.	はい	いいえ
l	The spider thread broke because of the weight of so many people.	はい	いいえ

4

Read the following conversation and write whether the speaker is male (男) or female (女) for each line. (*Hint:* take note of the end particles).

a **A:** いい天気だわ。ピクニックに行きましょうか。 ( )
B: そうだなあ。でも、ごごから雨がふるぞ。 ( )

b **A:** あの木の上にさるがいるぞ。木の上をはしることが上手だな。 ( )
B: ほんとうね。小さくてかわいいわね。 ( )

c **A:** おい、何をしているんだ。じゅぎょうがはじまるぞ。 ( )
B: 今、Eメールを書いているんだよ。じゅぎょうの前にぜんぶ書きたいんだ。 ( )

5

Circle the correct particle to complete the dialogues.

a **A:** 京子さん（**の、や、ね**）いちばん好きなテレビばんぐみ（**を、は、も**）何ですか。
B: サウスパーク（**を、が、で**）いちばん好きです。ひろしくん（**が、か、は**）?
A: ぼく（**も、の、を**）サウスパークが好きです。

b **A:** かずきくんはテニスをすることが上手だ（**ね、か、の**）。
B: ありがとう、毎日二時間れんしゅうする（**ね、んだ、か**）。将来テニスのせんしゅ（**の、に、は**）なりたいんだ。

c **A:** ロバートくんは、車（**を、は、で**）うんてんすること（**で、に、が**）できますか。
B: いいえ、ぼくはまだ十六才です。だから車をうんてんすることはできないんです（**か、よ、わ**）。

d **A:** この学校のコンピューターは新しくてはやいですね。昼休み（**に、や、の**）学校（**の、で、へ**）あと（**で、に、は**）インターネットをつかってもいいですか。
B: 昼休みはいいです。でも、学校のあとはだめですよ。

6

Categorise the following vocabulary and then colour code it accordingly: nouns *(red)*, verbs *(blue)*, adjectives *(yellow)* and phrases *(green)*. Then use the colour clues to make up sentences. Your sentences should all make sense and the same word can not be used more than once. Try some other examples in your exercise book.

Word bank

言う、くつ、せいふく、書く、かっこいい、まず、きびしい、きじ、水泳部、たとえば、すくない、先生、子どもの時、留学生、きそく、携帯電話、分かる、そうじする、将来、つかう、入る、一回、つぎ、わかい、らんぼうな、おそくなってごめんなさい、ぬぐ、はじまる、つく

yellow	red	blue
かっこいい	せいふくを	ぬがなければなりません。

a *green yellow red blue*

b *yellow yellow red blue*

c *green red blue*

Mock Test

/250

This test is made up of five sections: Kanji, Listening, Speaking, Reading and Writing. Each section totals 50 marks.

Kanji

/50

1

1x50= /

Change the following bolded kanji into hiragana (a–e) and vice versa (f–h).

a **毎朝**（　　　　　あさ）、**新聞**（　　　　　　）を**読**んで（　　　　　）、ラジオを
聞きます（　　　　　　　　）。

b **今週**（　　　　　　）、**新**しい（　　　　）**留学生**（りゅう　　　　　）が来ました。

c **来週**（らい　　　　）から**一週間**（　　　　　　　）、**私**（　　　　）の
家族（　　ぞく）は旅行に**出**かけます（　　　　　）。**冬休**み（　　　　み）の旅行です。

d **毎年**（　　　　　）**学校**（　　　　　　）に有**名**（ゆう　　　　）なスポーツ
せんしゅが来ます。

e **自**転**車**（　　てん　　）にのることが**下手**（　　　　）です。だから、
家（　　　　）から**高校**（　　　　）まであるいて行きます。

f **せんせい**（　　　　　　）、ペンフレンドに、誕**じょう日**（誕　　　　　）プレゼントを
おくります。**じゅう**所（　　　　　　　所）と**なまえ**（　　　　　　）をひらがなで
書いてください。

g いもうとは**しょうがくせい**（　　　　　　　　）で、時**どき**（時　　　　　）
しゅう末（　　　　末）に**て**紙（　　　　　紙）を書きます。

h **いりぐち**（　　　　　　）とドアの**あいだ**（　　　　　　）のはこに
じぶん（　　　　　）で**い**れて（　　　　　　）ください。

Listening

/50

1 ◎

/22

Listen to the conversation and answer the questions in English.

a Does Kenji still practise kendo? (2 marks)

____

b Give two reasons as to why Kenji no longer learning piano, English or dance? (2x2 marks)

(i) ______________________ **(ii)** ______________________

c What did Kyoko invite Kenji to do? When will she start? (2x2 marks)

____

d What other sporting activity does Kenji participate in? (2 marks)

____

e List the two training days and training times? (5 marks)

Day:	–	–	Day:	–

f Which training session can Kenji attend? Why? (2x2 marks)

____

g Did Kenji finally join the kendo club? (1 mark)

____

____

2 ◎ /28

Listen to the conversation and circle the correct answer. For *j* and *k* write your answer in Japanese.

a 恵(けい)子さんは本を読むことが好きですか。

はい	いいえ

b 恵(けい)子さんはどんな話(はなし)が好きですか。

ロマンス	アクション	まんが

c 恵(けい)子さんは大きくて、おもい本が好きですか。

はい	いいえ

d 恵(けい)子さんは月曜日から金曜日まで一日に何時間ぐらい本を読みますか。

1	2	3	12

e 週末(まつ)には、何時間ぐらい読みますか。

1	3	4	12

f 恵(けい)子さんはいつ本を読みますか。
(Circle two alternatives.)

じゅぎょうの前	じゅぎょうのあと
ばんごはんの前	ばんごはんのあと

g よしおくんは本を読むことが好きですか。

はい	いいえ

h よしおくんは一日に何時間ぐらいコンピューターゲームをしますか。

2	3	4	13

i よしおくんはいつコンピューターゲームをしますか。

ばんごはんの前	ばんごはんのあと

j よしおくんはばんごはんの前に何をしますか。(3 marks)

(i) ______________________

k どのぐらいしますか。(3 marks)

(i) ______________________

l よしおくんはテレビのアニメが好きですか。

はい	いいえ

Speaking

/50

1 

Study the personal profiles and choose one to prepare as a self-introduction.

a

Name: Jessica Lee
Age: 16
Year level: 10
Likes: playing hockey after school, drinking coke and eating ice-cream
Dislikes: watching TV before homework, school rules
Special ability: speaks Japanese, Indonesian, English and some French

b

Name: Samuel Jones
Age: 15
Year level: 10
Likes: computer games and karaoke, writing emails
Dislikes: writing letters, studying history
Special ability: plays guitar and belongs to a rock band

c

Name: Clare Roberts
Age: 16
Year level: 10
Likes: Japanese food, Hello Kitty, origami, talking with friends on the phone
Dislikes: running, studying in a noisy room, eating tofu and sashimi
Special ability: can write lots of kanji

Assessment criteria

- Pronunciation and intonation /5
- Fluency and phrasing /5
- Accuracy of language /5
- Memorisation /5
- Manner of delivery /5

TOTAL /25

2 

Part A Speaking

Find a partner in class and interview them by asking following questions in Japanese. Take notes and then write an informative essay about the person. Study the assessment criteria below.

Part B Writing

Your teacher may also want you to submit your essay on *genkooyooshi*. (refer to *Obentoo 2 Student Book* for the rules for using *genkooyooshi*.) Study the assessment criteria below.

a What is the name of the person?

b How many members are in his/her familiy? Who are they?

c How old s/he is or which year level is s/he in?

d Find out the details *(name, age, likes/dislikes)* of one member of her/his family.

e What sort of sports does s/he like playing?

f Does s/he like computers or books? What does s/he do in her/his spare time?

g How often *(How long)* does s/he do this activity?

h Does s/he like school? Does s/he belong to any clubs?

i What area/subject does s/he like studying?

j What does s/he want to be in the future?

Performance criteria

Part A Speaking

- Pronunciation and intonation /5
- Fluency and phrasing /5
- Accuracy of language /5
- Communicative skills /5
- Effectiveness /5

TOTAL /25

Part B Writing

- Content /5
- Suitability /5
- Range of language /5
- Accuracy of language /5
- Script /5

TOTAL /25

Reading

/50

1

2x5= /10

Write the number of the appropriate product (しょうひん) to match its description.

1	2	3	4	5
DVDプレーヤー	テレビ電話(わ)	カーナビシステム	ディスクマン	電子(し)オーガナイザー

a このしょうひんはすごいです。大きくてきれいです。でも、ぜんぜんおもくないです。だから、電車の中で、すぐつけることができます。学校のあとでのデートにべんりです。 ☐

b このしょうひんはすごいです。これは小さくてとてもべんりです。かばんの中に入れて、もって行くことができます。とてもきれいないろで、おもしろいおんがくが聞けます。 ☐

c このしょうひんはすごいです。新しいテクノロジーです。友(とも)だちのかおを見ることができます。このしょうひんはたくさんの電話(わ)ばんごうやメッセージをおぼえることができます。 ☐

d このしょうひんはすごいです。とても小さくて、あたまがよくてかっこいいです。シーディーやミニディスクや、フロッピーディスクをつかうことができます。 ☐

e このしょうひんはおもしろいです。車の中で、テレビスクリーンのちずを見ることができます。 ☐

2

2x10= /20

Daniela is hosting a Japanese student next month. She has asked you to help read the letter on the next page to answer her questions below in English.

a Why do you think Yuji is writing the letter in Japanese? ____________________

b What club does Yuji belong to? ____________________

c What does Yuji want to be in the future? ____________________

d How often does Yuji train? ____________________

e What does Yuji do every morning? ____________________

f What does Yuji want to do at Daniela's house? (2x2) ____________________

g List **two** other sports Yuji likes to do. **(i)** ____________ **(ii)** ____________

h What does Yuji want to do with Daniela in the summer? ____________________

i List **two** things Yuji says he will do after he has sent this letter. ____________________

j What did Yuji ask Daniela to do at the end of the letter? ____________________

単語表

なりたいです	want to become
おしえてあげます	I will teach you
おくってくれませんか	would you send me?

ダニエラさんへ、

手紙をどうもありがとうございました。ダニエラさんは、日本語がとても上手ですね。だから、ぼくは英語で手紙を書きません。ぼくは英語があんまり上手じゃないからです。

ぼくはサッカーぶに入っています。サッカーをすることが大好きです。ダニエラさんはサッカーが好きですか。ぼくのチームはとてもつよくて、日本で有名です。ぼくは将来プロのサッカーせんしゅになりたいです。ダニエラさんの家のちかくにこうえんがありますか。ぼくは毎日サッカーのれんしゅうをしなければなりません。それから、毎朝、あさごはんの前にジョギングもします。ダニエラさんの家でも、毎日ジョギングをしてもいいですか。

ぼくはおいしくてきれいなりょうりをすることが大好きです。だから、ダニエラさんの家で、いろいろな日本りょうりをつくりたいです。ダニエラさんとご家族はりょうりをすることが好きですか。ぼくがかんたんでおいしい日本りょうりをおしえてあげます。それから、ダニエラさんは水泳や、サーフィンをすることが好きですか。ぼくは、サーフィンをすることが上手です。水泳もよくします。プールに行ったり、海に行ったりします。オーストラリアはもうすぐ、夏ですね。ダニエラさんといっしょに海に行きたいです。

それじゃあ、お手紙をまっています。この手紙のあとで、ダニエラさんにEメールを書きます。読んでください。ぼくのしゃしんもEメールでおくります。ダニエラさんとご家族のしゃしんをEメールでおくってくれませんか。ダニエラさんに会えることをとてもたのしみにしています。さようなら。

十一月十日　　　　ゆうじより

3

5X4=　　/20

Give the meanings of the sentences in English.

a 日本の新聞はかんじがたくさんあって、とてもむずかしいです。でも、私は毎日読むことが好きです。

____

____

b 私の家族は先月ひっこししました。家は新しくてとてもきれいです。だから、家でくつをはいてはだめです。

____

____

c 私のスポーツクラブにはいろいろなきそくがあります。れんしゅうの前にじゅんびたいそうをしなければなりません。それから、しあいのあとで、日記を書かなければなりません。

____

____

d 二年前に、一人でヨーロッパに行って、とてもたのしかったです。しゃしんをたくさんとることができました。今度(こんど)アメリカに行きたいです。

Writing

1

2x2.5+4x5= /25

Your friend Sally is hosting Kayo, a Japanese student. Sally can't come to school today and so she has asked you to look after Kayo for the day. Kayo has been at your school for a week but has not been to your classes before. Explain the following phrases in Japanese.

During English (5 marks)

a "You must not speak in Japanese, Kayo."

b "You must write about your school in English in your exercise book, Kayo."

During geography (10 marks)

c "Kayo, can you draw a map (ちず) of Australia?"

d "Kayo, you may use pencils and a ruler. Here you are!"

At lunchtime (10 marks)

e "Kayo, we are not allowed to eat in the classroom. Let's go outside and talk to my friends, Jenny and Tanya."

f "Look at this magazine, Kayo. This comic is cute and interesting. Do you like reading comics?"

2

You are to write an e-mail to a Japanese exchange student who will be coming to your school. Write three or four sentences about the topics listed below. There are several ways to present your work. Ask your teacher.

- If you have access to a computer with a Japanese program, send the email to your teacher.
- Alternatively, if your teacher wishes to do this under test conditions, write your email below. The length should be 100–200 characters, which includes the beginning and ending similar to a letter format.

Topics

- self-introduction *(name, age, year level, where you live, family etc)*
- sports and interests *(what you like/dislike, what you are good/not good at, free time activities/hobbies, when and how long you do it, reasons etc.)*
- your school *(school rules, uniform, club activities, how you get to school etc.)*

Assessment criteria

- Content /5
- Suitability * /5
- Variety of sentence structures and vocabulary /5
- Accuracy of language /5
- Script /5

TOTAL /25

* depending on type of submission

5 アルバイト

1

Answer the following questions in English.

a Do you have a part-time job? If so, describe your part-time job.

b What kind of jobs in your country require Japanese language skills?

c What do you need to prepare before you apply for a job?

d What kind of jobs would you like do if you had the opportunity to work in Japan?

2

Refer to the Unit 5 漢字の書き方 on page 134 for the stroke order practice of the kanji introduced in this unit. There are also reading and writing exercises and a game or puzzle for you to practise the new kanji.

3

Give the English equivalent for the Japanese or the Japanese equivalent for the English.

a 電子辞書 ______

b せいせき ______

c 会話 ______

d 貿易会社 ______

e むすめ ______

f いる ______

g part-time job ______

h tutor ______

i shop assistant ______

j guide ______

k hospital ______

l interview ______

m job ______

n future ______

o report card ______

p hourly wage ______

4

You will be asked to listen and/or read the 会話 in the Student Book on page 77 and number the phrases below in the correct order .

- a ☐ ジョンさんは西村(にしむら)さんに電話しました。
- b ☐ 西村(にしむら)さんはジョンさんに電話しました。
- c ☐ ジョンさんは日本人の留(りゅう)学生について話しました。
- d ☐ ジョンさんは西村(にしむら)さんの家にめんせつに行きました。
- e ☐ 西村(にしむら)さんはアルバイトの時間とその時給(きゅう)について話しました。
- f ☐ ジョンさんはかえりました。
- g ☐ 西村(にしむら)さんはむすめの雪子さんをしょうかいしました。
- h ☐ ジョンさんは学校としゅみについて話しました。
- i ☐ 雪子さんは英(えい)語のべんきょうについて話しました。

5

Match the Japanese sentence with its English equivalent by writing the sentence number. Then underline the English word that means から in Japanese.

1 I will not go to school because the weather is bad.

2 I can not telephone since I do not have a mobile phone.

3 My brother can not speak as he is still only one year old.

- a 天気がわるいですから、学校に行きません。 ☐
- b おとうとはまだ一才(さい)ですから、話すことができません。 ☐
- c 携帯(けいたい)電話をもっていませんから、電話できません。 ☐

6

Listen and tick the correct reason and consequence for each scenario.

	Reasons		Consequences	
a				
b			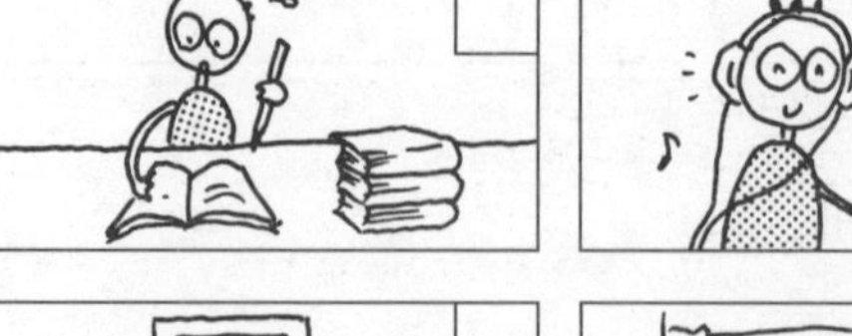	
c				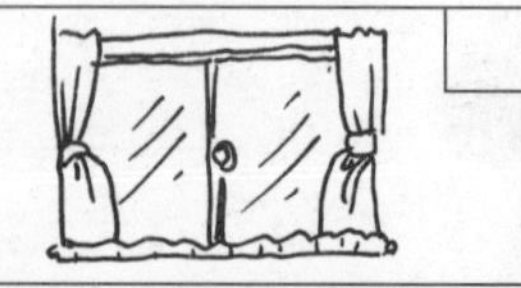

7

Look at the English clues and the pairs of Japanese sentences. Work out which sentence shows the reason and which shows the consequence. Number the reason as 1 and the consequence as 2 because this is the order when you make a sentence in Japanese using から. Combine the sentences using から、and write your new sentence in the space below.

a Kate did not go to school yesterday because she was sick.

ケイトさんは病(びょう)気でした。 (　　)

きのう学校に行きませんでした。 (　　)

____

b I will have a hot cup of coffee because it is very cold today.

あついコーヒーを飲(の)みます。 (　　)

今日はとてもさむいです。 (　　)

____

c I must practise golf because I am not very good at it.

ゴルフがあんまり上手じゃないです。 (　　)

れんしゅうしなければなりません。 (　　)

____

d I will study Japanese more because I want to go to Japan next year.

来年日本に行きたいです。 (　　)

もっと日本語をべんきょうします。 (　　)

____

8

Do you remember from *Obentoo 2* that から can be used at the end of the sentence when you are responding to どうして or なぜ (*Why?*)? A Japanese student who is visiting your class wants to know lots of information about you. Answer the questions in Japanese using から at the end of the sentence. Take it in turns to answer and respond.

a どうしてきのう学校に来ませんでしたか。

b どうしてコーラをたくさん飲(の)みますか。

c どうしてせいふくをきていませんか。

d どうしてばんごはんを食べませんか。

e どうしてあのへやに入ってはだめですか。

f どうしてテレビを見ませんか。

9

Listen and highlight the speaker's reason.

a
Because he had soccer practice.
Because he was playing a TV game.
Because he had a maths test.

b
Because she was playing in the snow.
Because she was inside the shopping centre.
Because she was inside at home.

c Because she likes eating.
Because she likes cooking and eating.
Because she likes cooking and talking to customers.

d Because he left his dictionary at school.
Because he went out with his friend.
Because he left his Japanese books at school.

e Because the bus came early.
Because the computer was not working.
Because he did not want to go to the interview.

10

John and Derrick are discussing what to take for some proposed activities. Listen and tick the items which are necessary and a cross for the unnecessary items.

a

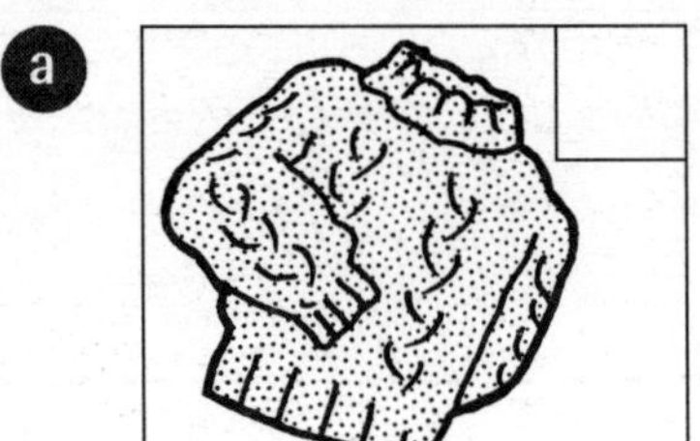

b

c

d

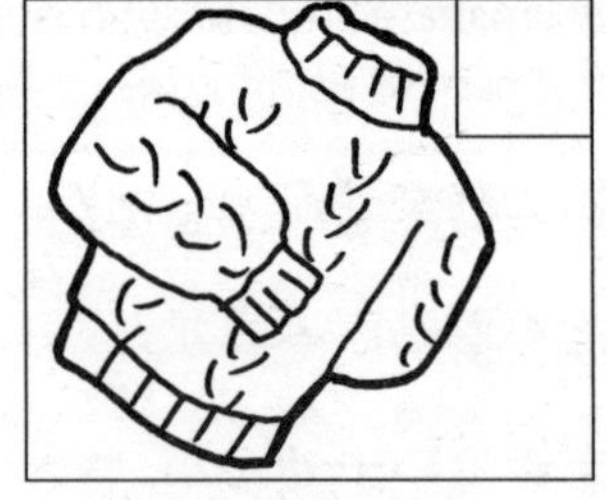

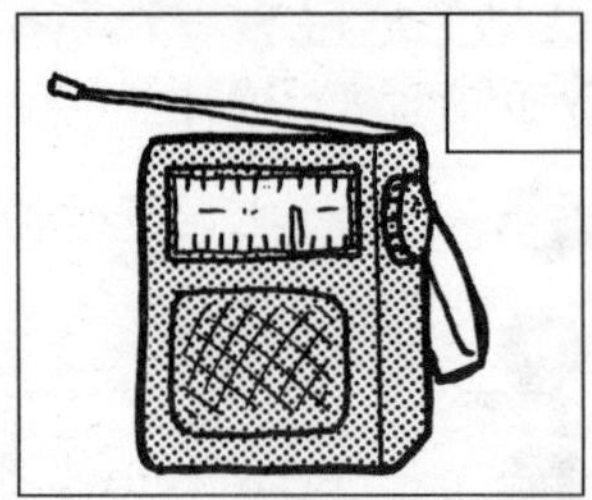

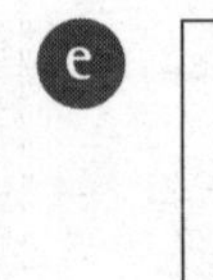

e

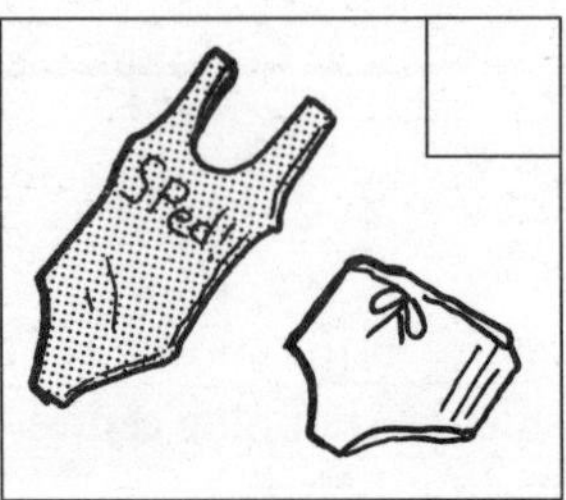

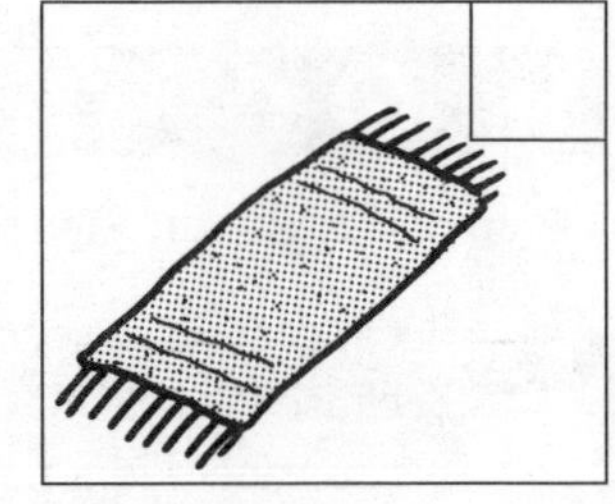

11 

You and your friend are planing to go on a holiday. With your partner decide what you need or you do not need to take using the items below.

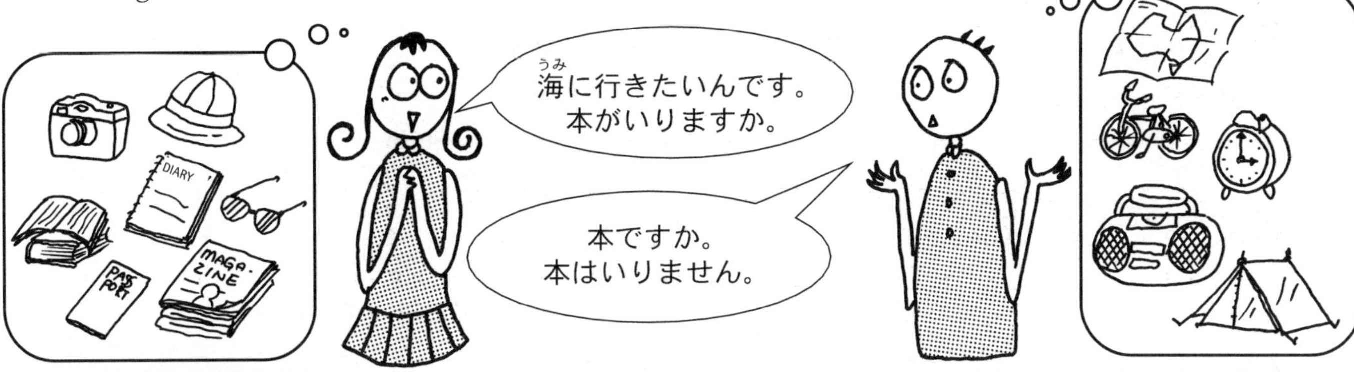

DIARY
MAGA-ZINE
PASSPORT
海に行きたいんです。本がいりますか。
本ですか。本はいりません。

12

Read the statements to guess the jobs in English.

a

九時から六時まではたらきます。土曜日がいちばんいそがしいです。木曜日は九時まではたらきます。はさみがいります。よく人と話します。ドライヤーをよくつかいます。そうぞうりょくがいります。

はさみ scissors
そうぞうりょく creativity

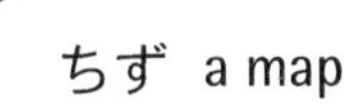

b

四時から十時まではたらきます。金曜日と土曜日がいちばんいそがしいです。うんてんめんきょがいります。安いピザを食べることができます。ちずがいります。いつもお金をもっています。

c

月曜日から金曜までのあさ五時から十時まではたらきます。いつもいろいろな新聞を読んで、せかいのニュースをべんきょうしなければなりません。テレビに出ますから、きれいなスーツがたくさんいります。有名な人にインタビューをします。

せかい world
出る to appear

d

月曜日から金曜日までのあさ六時から四時まではたらきます。時々土曜日にもはたらきます。家にのぼってペンキをぬります。それから、のこぎりで木をきります。しごとはおもしろいです。でも、すこしあぶないですから、じょうぶなふくとくつがいります。

ペンキ	paint
ぬる	to paint
のこぎり	a saw
きる	to cut
じょうぶな	sturdy

13

This is a role-play between a person who has recently been to a job interview *(Student A)* and a person who is going for an interview for a shop assistant's job *(Student B)*.

Student A	Student B
Ask when the interview is.	
	Say it is on Saturday at 10 o'clock. Find out what you have to do before the interview.
Say you must practise for the interview and you need a CV and a school report.	
	Say you have them all. Ask her/him to ask you some questions.
Find out why s/he has applied for the job.	
	Because you like to talk to people and you want to use your Japanese.
Ask which day can s/he work.	
	Say you can work from 4 o'clock on Monday, Wednesday, Thursday and on the weekend.
Ask why s/he can't work on Tuesdays.	
	Say because you go to karate class every Tuesday.
Ask if s/he can come after karate on Tuesday.	
	Say you can't because karate is until 9 o'clock.
Ask if s/he can work Thursdays and the weekend.	
	Accept the offer and find out the hourly wage.
It's nine dollars per hour.	
	Accept.
Farewell.	
	Show appreciation.

14

Listen to the conversations where people are talking about what they want to buy using their savings from their part-time jobs. Note down their responses in English.

a ______________________________

b ______________________________

c ______________________________

d ______________________________

e ______________________________

f ______________________________

15

Rearrange the Japanese words to make the sentences. Check that the meaning corresponds with the English given.

a I want a new computer because my family's computer is old.
(私の家族（ぞく）の、新しい、が、ふるい、ほしいです。コンピューターは、コンピューター、から、が、です。)

b I want an electronic dictionary and money for my birthday present.
(ほしい、が、電子辞書（じしょ）、誕生日（たんじょうび）、に、と、です。、プレゼント、お金)

c I want a new bag and a blue dress because my friend and I will go to the party tomorrow.
(ほしいです。明日（あした）、に、パーティー、から、私、新しい、と、かばん、友（とも）だちと、あおい、は、行きます、が、ドレス)

d Last year I wanted a snowboard for a Christmas present.
(クリスマス、に、スノーボード、ほしかった、が、プレゼント、です。、去年（きょねん）)

e Do you want a Pokemon book and a video tape?
(ビデオテープ、が、ポケモン、本、と、か、の、ほしいです。)

16

Jane is going to Tokyo and she wants to visit Tokyo Disneyland. She sent an email to her friend, Sachiyo to explain what she wants to see and do there. In your exercise book, note down as many of Jane's wishes as you can.

さちよさん、

Eメールどうもありがとう。ディズニーランドでいろいろなことをしたいです。
まず、ミッキーマウスのぬいぐるみがほしいです。スペースマウンテンにのりたいです。
ミニーマウスのぼうしがほしいです。アドベンチャーランドで、ジャングルクルーズにのりたいです。アイスクリームと、ドーナッツがほしいです。ビッグサンダーマウンテンにのりたいです。スモールワールドと、スターツアーズに行きたいです。ディズニーランドのクッキーがほしいです。ハンバーガーが食（た）べたいです。ミッキーマウスとドナルドダックといっしょにしゃしんをとりたいです。ライオンキングのマウスパッドがほしいです。
パレードを見たいです。くまのプーさんのマグカップがほしいです。カヌーにのりたいです。

じゃあね、ジェーン

17

Part A

Survey six members of your class by asking them the following questions. Record their responses on the chart.

将来（しょうらい）、何になりたいですか。

どうして（なぜ）～になりたいですか。

Name			
Job			
Why?			

Name			
Job			
Why?			

What is the most popular future occupation in the class? ______________________________

Part B

Using the information from **Part A**, write a profile in Japanese of one of the students who you interviewed. You will need to ask her/him a few more questions to complete the profile. Note down the extra questions below and record his/her responses. Present your written profile on *genkooyooshi*.

Revise the rules for using *genkooyooshi.*

18

Natalie has been studying Japanese for more than three years. She has just returned from a job interview for a waitress at a Japanese restaurant. She is very excited and has described her interview in her diary. Complete the chart in English according to what she has written.

八月三日　月曜日　雨

今日、日本レストランのアルバイトのめんせつに行った。レストランはとてもきれいで、おきゃくさんがたくさんいた。レストランは家からちかかったから、あるいて十五分ぐらいで行くことができた。

めんせつで、レストランのマネージャーが日本語でいろいろなことを聞いた。私のしゅみや、好きなりょうりについてなどだった。私はいっしょうけんめい日本語でこたえた。時給は８ドル７５セントだから、あんまりわるくない。私は、アルバイトのお金で新しいCDプレーヤーが買いたい。今の自転車はふるいから、かっこいい自転車もほしい。ようふくや、かわいいかばんやアクセサリーもほしい。

今週の木曜日からしごとがはじまる。レストランで、きものをきなければならない。それから、げたもはかなければならない。きものはとてもすてきだ。でも、ちょっとはずかしい。しごとで、おけしょうをしなければならない。私は、おけしょうがあんまり好きじゃないから、すこしいやだ。それから、かみがながいから、ヘアクリップで、かみをとめなければならない。

レストランのしごとはとてもいそがしいから、ほかのウエートレスと話してはだめだ。だから、アルバイトの前にメニューをぜんぶおぼえなければならない。大変だ。しごとで、小さいエプロンがいる。それから、ペンやノートがいる。しごとの前に、ほかのウエートレスにいろいろなことを聞かなければならない。私のはじめてのアルバイトだから、いっしょうけんめいはたらきたい。

とめなければならない
must hold

She wants	She must	She must not	She needs

19

Read the cover letter George wrote to attach to his CV for a job application. Answer the questions in English.

日本観光旅行会社
人事担当者
ピーター・キンドラーさま

私は、エルトロ高校の一年生のジョージ・サンダーソンです。私は旅行が大好きですから、旅行会社ではたらきたいです。

エルトロ高校で四年間日本語をべんきょうしました。日本語でかんたんな会話をすることができます。それから、ひらがなとカタカナと漢字が書けますから、みじかいさくぶんも書くことができます。また、かんたんなガイドブックや、手紙も読むことができます。私は三年前から、日本のペンフレンドに手紙を書いています。さいきんは、Eメールも書きます。ペンフレンドの名前は、寺西よしおくんと言います。よしおくんも旅行が好きですから、私たちはよく日本や、アメリカや、オーストラリアや、ヨーロッパなどのかんこうちについて手紙で話します。

私の学校と、よしおくんの学校は、シスタースクールですから、日本人の生徒が毎年エルトロ高校に来ます。今年日本人の生徒がエルトロ高校の先生や友だちといっしょに動物園や、かんこうちに行きました。そして、私はいつも、日本語で動物やかんこうちについてせつめいしました。私は、日本語で私の町について話すことが大好きです。

将来、かんこうガイドになりたいです。そして、いろいろなところを日本人にしょうかいしたいです。いっしょうけんめいしごとをします。よろしくおねがいします。

十月十五日

ジョージ・サンダーソン より

単語表

かんこうち	sightseeing spots
せつめいする	to explain
かんこうガイド	tour guide
しょうかいする	to introduce

a. George is applying for the position of a:
- Japanese teacher
- tour guide
- telephone operator

b. What are his Japanese skills like?

____

c. How long has George had a penpal? How do they communicate?

____

d. What did he do together with the Japanese students from his sister school?

____

e. What does he want to do in the future?

____

20

Answer each question and move down the chart to find out what the fortune teller's job advice is for you in the future.

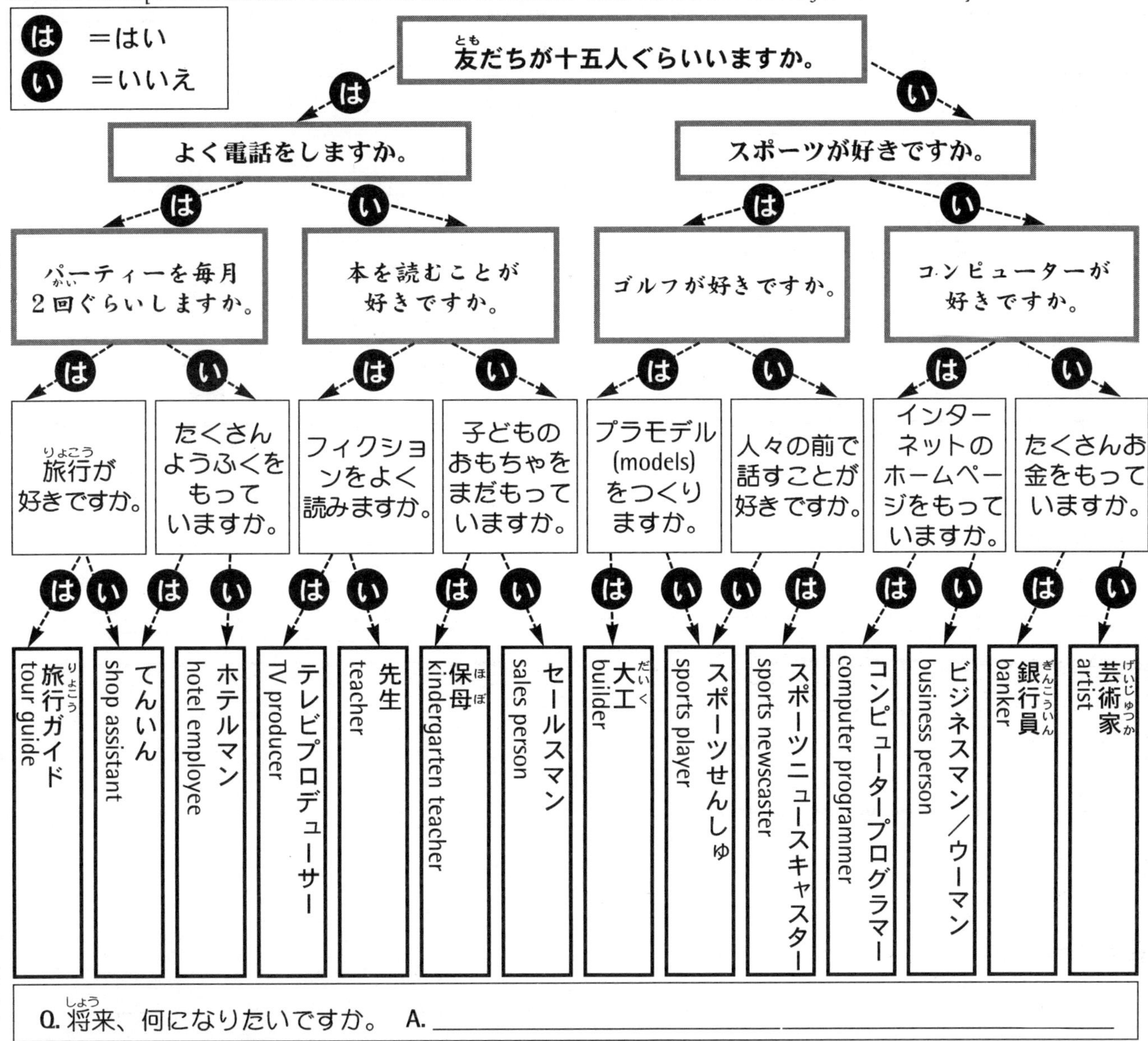

は =はい
い =いいえ
友だちが十五人ぐらいいますか。
よく電話をしますか。
スポーツが好きですか。
パーティーを毎月2回ぐらいしますか。
本を読むことが好きですか。
ゴルフが好きですか。
コンピューターが好きですか。
旅行が好きですか。
たくさんようふくをもっていますか。
フィクションをよく読みますか。
子どものおもちゃをまだもっていますか。
プラモデル (models) をつくりますか。
人々の前で話すことが好きですか。
インターネットのホームページをもっていますか。
たくさんお金をもっていますか。
旅行ガイド tour guide
てんいん shop assistant
ホテルマン hotel employee
テレビプロデューサー TV producer
先生 teacher
保母 kindergarten teacher
セールスマン sales person
大工 builder
スポーツせんしゅ sports player
スポーツニュースキャスター sports newscaster
コンピュータープログラマー computer programmer
ビジネスマン／ウーマン business person
銀行員 banker
芸術家 artist

Q. 将来、何になりたいですか。 A. ____________________

21

Listen to 見る 聞く 分かる on page 88 of your Student Book. Using the information from Lina's interview with Masako, note down the main points you hear.

Lina's questions

正子さんは日本にいましたか。
正子さんはどんなアルバイトをしましたか。
しごとはたのしかったですか。
毎週何回ぐらいアルバイトをしましたか。
何時から何時までしましたか。
時給はいくらでしたか。
アルバイトのお金を何につかいましたか。
友だちもアルバイトをしていましたか。

Masako's responses

22

Using the sample CV in your Student Book on pages 86–7, write your own CV on this Japanese りれきしょ.

履歴書　平成　年　月　げんざい	しゃしん
ふりがな　※男・女	
氏名　いん	
※　昭和　年　月　日生　本籍 平成　（まん　さい）	
ふりがな　〒	
じゅうしょ	電話番号

年	月	学歴·職歴
		学歴
		職歴

好きなかもく	けんこうじょうたい

しゅみ	しぼうのどうき

スポーツ

本人希望記入欄

家族氏名	せいべつ	年齢	家族氏名	せいべつ	年齢

つうきん時間	扶養家族 人	配偶者 ※有・無

ほごしゃ ふりがな	電話 〒
氏名	じゅうしょ

23

Read the job advertisements to complete the tasks.

英語の家庭教師

日本語が上手な人。１５～１８才。
日本語が上手な人。１５～１８才。中学２年生のむすめに英語をおしえてください。
時給は、千二百円です。
一週間に１回家に来てください。
電話番号：０４１７　５４０　９１２

ウエイター・ウエイトレス

日本語が上手で、あかるいせいかくの人。
日本レストラン。
16才から30才ぐらいまで。
金曜日と土曜日と日曜日の5時から10時まではたらけますか。時給は830円です。
電話番号　9764　8011

サッカーのコーチ

日本語が話せて、サッカーが上手な人。
日本人の子どもにサッカーをおしえてください。
子どもは八才から十五才までです。れんしゅうは一週間に一回、土曜日の九時から十二時までです。
時給は６８０円です。
9531 8540の「さかもと」に電話してください。

ツアーガイド

日本語が上手で、旅行が好きな人。
(日本語のテストがあります。)
１６～３０才。
夏と冬は一週間に３日、春と秋は毎日しごとがあります。
時給は３０００円です。
電話番号：0419 383 657

てんいん

日本語が上手で、ようふくが好きな人。
15才から17才ぐらいまで。町のブティックではたらきます。一週間に３日から５日はたらいてください。
時給：７００円。
電話番号：9436-5128

Part A

Write a cover letter for your application for a part-time job for one of the advertisements above. Task 19 may assist you with your application. You might include:

- reason(s) for applying
- future plans and aspirations
- previous work experience
- relevant studies

Part B

You have received the following interview questions before the interview. With a partner, simulate the job interview. Before you begin, study the assessment criteria. The interviewer who is also the assessor will give you a score according to the criteria (1= very weak to 5 = very strong) and any other relevant comments. Try to include extra, interesting information in your responses and to show your enthusiasm toward the job. Then swap roles.

自己紹介(こしょうかい)をしてください。

どうしてこのアルバイトをしたいと思(おも)いましたか。

これがはじめてのアルバイトですか。今までどんなアルバイトをしましたか。

どこで日本語をべんきょうしましたか。どのぐらいべんきょうしていますか。

しゅみは何ですか。

どんなしごとができますか。

将(しょう)来、何になりたいですか。

週に何日はたらくことができますか。何時から何時まではたらけますか。

時給(きゅう)は～ですが、いいですか。

何かしつもんがありますか。

Assessment criteria

- interest in job
- capabilities for job
- personality
- sense of responsibility
- Japanese language skills *(relevant to the job)*
- negotiation of work times
- acceptance of wage
- basic social communication skills *(delivery method)*

/40

24

Have fun by making a 名刺(めいし) on your computer/word processor. You can make a 名刺(めいし) to use now and also an imaginative 名刺(めいし) to use when you start working in the near future. Produce your 名刺(めいし) with Japanese on one side and English on the other side. Refer to your Student Book on page 90 for further details. The standard size of a 名刺(めいし) is 9cm x 5.5cm.

25

Research one or more of the following topics. Try using a variety of sources including the internet. You might also like to compare the Japanese experience to your own country.

- Japanese working conditions *(working hours, holidays, wages, working conditions, women in the workforce etc.)*
- commuting hours in Japan
- where to look for jobs available in Japan or for Japanese speakers
- Japanese businesses overseas
- part-time and full-time jobs in Japan

おべんとうクイズ

1 Match the Japanese word with its English equivalent.

ガイド •	• teacher
時給(きゅう) •	• hospital
会社員(しゃいん) •	• suit
貿易会社(ぼうえきしゃ) •	• job
きょうし •	• professional golfer
カメラマン •	• hourly wages
びょういん •	• trading company
てんいん •	• company employee
プロゴルファー •	• guide
しごと •	• shop assistant
スーツ •	• camera operator

2 Write the following kanji words in hiragana and write their meanings.

a 英会話　えい____________________

b 電話　____________________

c 辞書　じ____________________

d 社会　しゃ____________________

e 将来　しょう____________________

f 会います　____________________

g お母さん　____________________

h 外国語　がいこく____________________

3 Complete the following sentences by adding the appropriate kanji words and check you know the meaning of the sentences in English.

a じゅんくんの__________(おとうさん)は____________(えいご)が上手です。

b ________社(かいしゃ)でアルバイトをして、レポートの________き方(かきかた)をならいました。

c オーストラリアでは________(ははのひ)は五月、__________(ちちのひ)は九月にあります。

d ________(らいげつ)、日本から留(りゅう)学生が来ますから、__________(にほんご)をいっしょうけんめいべんきょうします。

e 子どもがねていますから、しずかに__________(はなして)ください。

4 Join the two sentences by using から *(because)*. Check they are in the appropriate order.

a 日本語が大好きです。毎日、日本語をべんきょうします。

____

____

b レストランに行きましょう。すしが食(た)べたいです。

____

____

c トレーニングをしなければなりません。やきゅうせんしゅです。

____

____

d 昨日(きのう)よくねられませんでした。今日ははやくねたいです。

____

____

5 Respond to each question by saying three items in Japanese.

a 車をうんてんしたいです。何がいりますか。

b すしをつくりたいです。何がいりますか。

c 海(うみ)に行って、ビーチバレーボールをしたいです。何がいりますか。

d 山でキャンプがしたいです。何がいりますか。

6 How would you respond to the following questions?

a クリスマスプレゼントに何がほしいですか。

b 誕生日(たんじょう)に何がほしいですか。

c バレンタインデーに何がほしいですか。

7 Survey five people in your class to find out what they want to be in the future. Jot down their answers below.

a ______________________________

b ______________________________

c ______________________________

d ______________________________

e ______________________________

8 Read the following article written by an Australian who lived in Japan for a year. Answer the questions in English.

私は日本の会社ではたらきたかったです。私は日本に留学して、日本の大学に一年間かよいました。大学では、いつも日本語で話さなければなりませんでした。でも、はじめは日本語があんまりできなかったから、英語の家庭教師をしました。時給はあんまり高くなかったですが、日本語をならうことができました。このしごとはとてもよかったです。

家庭教師のあとで、ざっしのモデルをしました。モデルの時給はとてもよくて、二千円でした。私は、たくさんの日本語の本や、電子辞書がほしかったから、ながい時間しごとをしました。いろいろなモデルクラブに入って、毎週週末にはたらきました。モデルクラブには、オーストラリア人や、アメリカ人や、カナダ人や、イギリス人がたくさんいて、私はよく英語で話しました。でも、もっと日本語を話したかったから、モデルクラブをやめて、会社ではたらきました。

その会社は大きい貿易会社で、たくさんの会社員がいました。私はそこで、英語をつかって、しごとをしました。英語のしごとがおおかったですが、私は将来会社員になりたかったから、とてもいいしごとだと思いました。今は日本の貿易会社に入って、オーストラリアではたらいています。日本でのアルバイトがとてもいいけいけんになりました。

a List his three jobs *(in sequence).*

____

____

b Why did he do the first job?

____

c Describe the working conditions of his first job.

____

d What was the wage for the second job and when did he work?

____

e Why did he work long hours for the second job?

____

f Why did he quit his second job?

____

g Why did he think the third job was good for him?

____

9 If you have a part-time job, write a description in Japanese as an informative article. If you don't work, write about a possible future job or simply a job you would like to have.

The article should/may include:

- Description of the job *(what you do, what you are not allowed to do)*
- Hours of work
- Commuting time
- Salary
- Description of the people you work with
- Your impression *(feeling)* about the job
- What you want to do in the future or how you are spending your salary

Length: 150 - 200 字
(a sheet of げんこうようし is 400 字)

Audience: Job seekers

Style: Informative

やめる	quit
いいけいけんになる	to become a good experience

6 日本旅行(りょこう)

1

Answer the questions in English. You might like to discuss some of your responses with a partner.

- **a** Have you ever been to Japan or have you ever met someone from Japan?
- **b** What places in Japan have you heard of?
- **c** Do you know which Japanese city was the capital before Tokyo?
- **d** If you were going to Japan for a holiday, where would you go?
- **e** Do you know what an おんせん、神社(じんじゃ) and おてら are?
- **f** What are the different ways you can travel around Japan and where can you stay?

2

Refer to the Unit 6 漢字(かんじ)の書き方(かた) on page 138 for the stroke order practice of the kanji introduced in this unit. There are also reading and writing exercises and a game or puzzle for you to practise the new kanji.

3

You had sorted your travel flashcards into three groups (transport, action words and places) but your younger brother has mixed them up! See how quickly you can reorganise them by completing the table.

くうこう　かど　みせ　見える　車
あんないする　タクシー　旅行(りょ)する　のりかえる　おてら
地下鉄(ちかてつ)　はし　バス　電車　かかる
おみやげや　飛行機(ひこうき)　まがる　聞く　神社(じんじゃ)
新幹線(かんせん)　まっすぐ行く　ふね　わたる　舞子(まいこ)

Find the odd word out and its meaning.

Transport	Action words	Places

4

Michael has just returned from an exchange trip to Japan and he has prepared a speech to give his class. Listen and complete the tasks below.

Part A

As you listen to Michael's speech, fill in the details in Japanese.

	春休み	夏休み	九月
どこ？			
何をした？			
だれと？			

いちばんたのしかったところはどこでしたか。____________________

Part B

Prepare some questions to ask Michael about his experience.

a ____________________

b ____________________

c ____________________

d ____________________

5

You will be asked to listen and/or read the 会話 of your Student Book on pages 95–7. Mark each statement either ○ or ×.

a たけしくんとセーラさんは自由行動があるから、京都を見物しています。 ☐

b たけしくん: おみやげの買い物をしたいんです。 ☐

c 京都では、祇園と四条で買い物ができます。 ☐

d 竜安寺から祇園までバスで行きます。 ☐

e 舞子さんはきものをきません。 ☐

f むかし、京都は日本のしゅとでした。 ☐

6

Listen to the dialogues and in Japanese record where the speakers want to go and how long it will take to get to there from 大阪(さか).

	どこに行きたい？	どのぐらいかかる？
a		
b		
c		
d		

7

With a partner, answer the questions in Japanese about travelling to places from your home. *(If you are unsure of the answer, estimate!)*

> **A:** 家からスーパーまで、どのぐらいかかりますか。
>
> **B:** 車で五分かかります。

a 家からえきまで、車でどのぐらいかかりますか。

b 家からゆうびんきょくまで、どのぐらいかかりますか。

c 家から友(とも)だちの家まで、どのぐらいかかりますか。

d 家から学校まで、どうやっていきますか。
どのぐらいかかりますか。

8

Jenny is keeping a record in her notebook in Japanese of how long it took to get to various places during her 修学旅行(しゅうりょ). In your exercise book, write each sentence in Japanese.

a 2 hours and 30 minutes by shinkansen from Tokyo to Kyoto

b 1 hour on foot from the hotel to Kiyomizu dera

c 30 minutes by bus from Shijo to Kinkakuji

d 40 minutes by train from Kyoto to Nara

e 10 minutes by subway from the station to the hotel

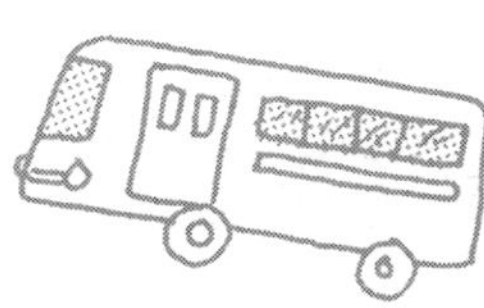

9

Listen to the following people ask the travel agent for the time it will take to travel between various places in Japan. Note down in Japanese where they want to go, the mode of transport they plan to use and how long it will take in each situation.

	どこに行く？	何で行く？	どのぐらいかかる？
a			
b			
c			
d			

10

Where will the following people end up? Listen to the three sets of directions given and trace the paths on the map. Start at the information booth each time. Write the letter of the dialogue at each destination.

On the map of this town you will notice there aren't any street names or numbers in Japan. If you don't know why, ask your teacher.

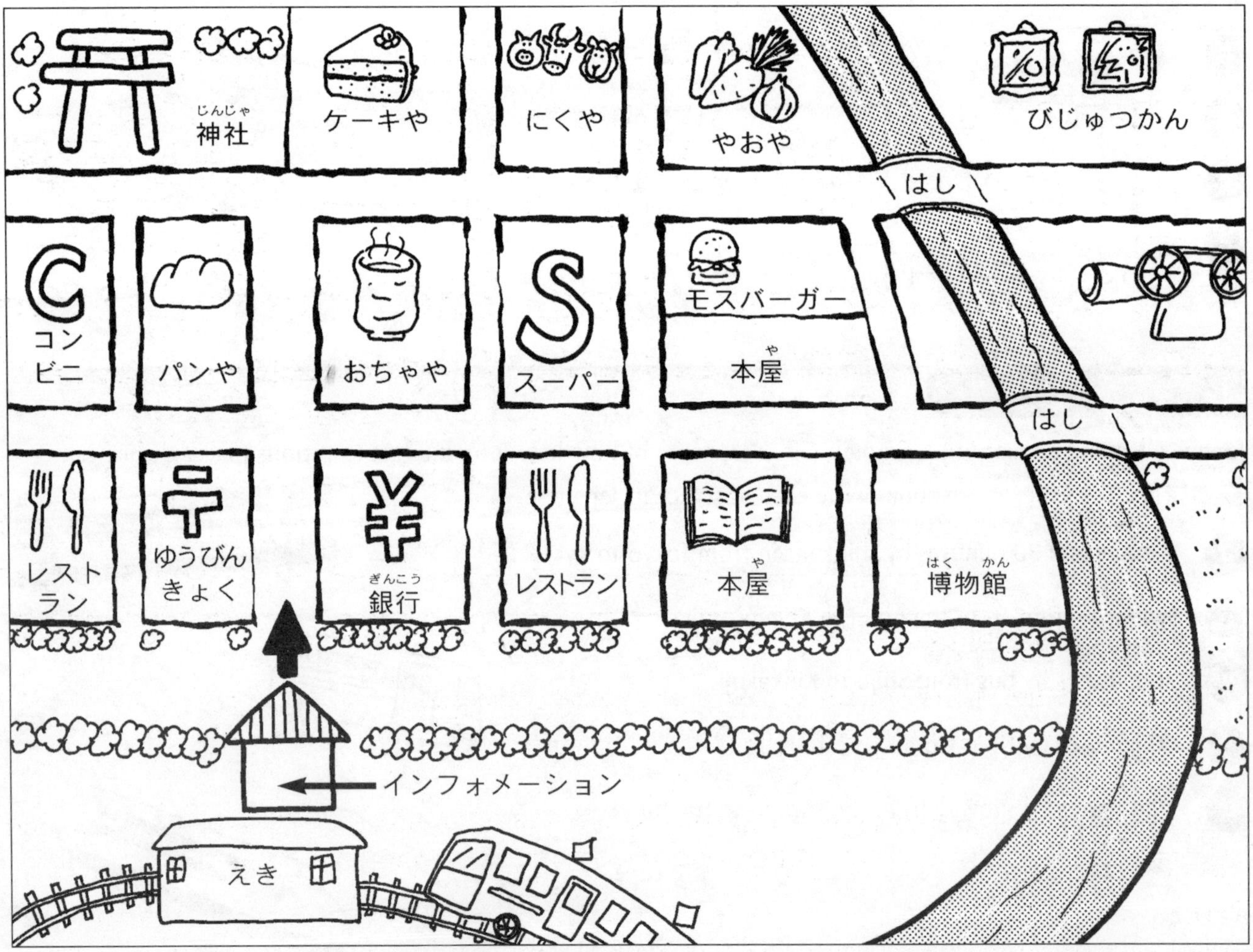

神社
ケーキや
にくや
やおや
びじゅつかん
はし
コンビニ
パンや
おちゃや
スーパー
モスバーガー
本屋
はし
レストラン
ゆうびんきょく
銀行
レストラン
本屋
博物館
インフォメーション
えき

11

The hotel concierge has written down some instructions for you to get to a number of places from the hotel. Read them and trace the directions on the town map.
You are in the hotel lobby.

- ホテルを出て、右にまがって、まっすぐ行ってください。三つめのかどを左にまがって、つぎのかどを右にまがって、ちょっと行くと、右側にあります。そこで、おいしい物が買えます。
- ホテルを出て、右にまがって、まっすぐ行ってください。つぎのかどを左にまがります。まっすぐ行って、つぎのこうさてんを左にまがってください。右側にあります。
- ホテルを出て、右にまがって、三つ目のかどを右にまがってください。すこし行って、しんごうをわたると、右側にあります。そこでいろいろな物が見られます。

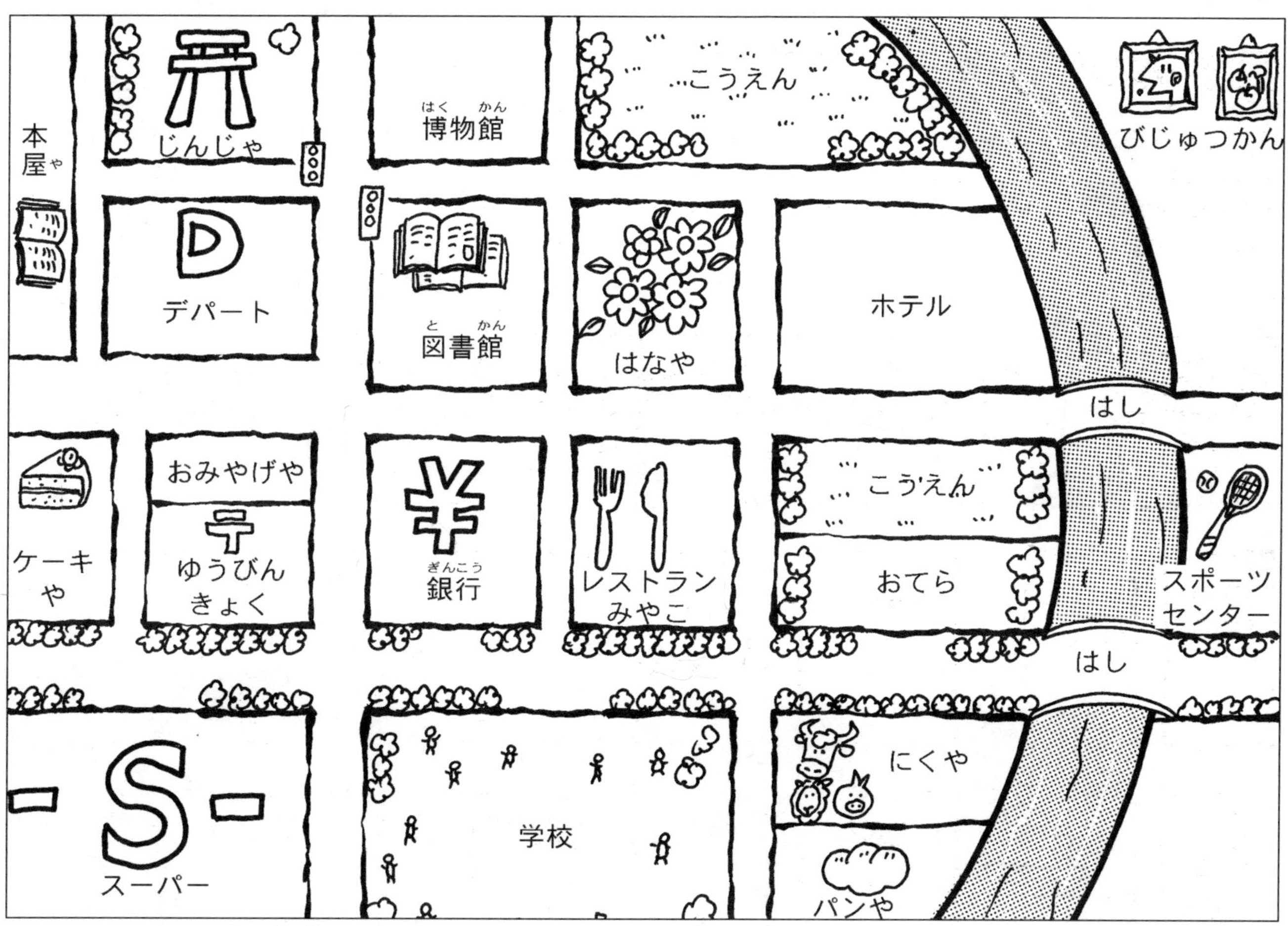

12

A visiting student from Japan wants to get around your town by herself. Decide on five places you think are important *(i.e. supermarket, post office, bus stop closest to her house etc.)*.

Part A

In Japanese, write directions from your school to the five places you have chosen. On a sheet of paper or in your exercise book, draw a map and label it appropriately to assist with your explanation.

Part B

With a partner, prepare a dialogue based on this situation. One person will need to take the role of the exchange student.

13

With a partner, choose a secret location and write out a set of instructions on how to get there. You should try to include at least ten instructions. On a separate sheet of paper prepare a map showing the starting point. When you have finished, show your map to another pair for them to guess the secret location. They will ask questions like まっすぐ行きますか。右にまがりますか。つぎのかどをどちらにまがりますか。 You respond appropriately in Japanese to let them know whether they are going the right way or not, until they find the location.

Here are some useful phrases. You may be able to think of some others.

はい、そうです。

はい、まっすぐ行ってください。

はい、右にまがってください。

いいえ、ちがいます。

How quickly can they find the secret location?

14

Listen to the directions and number the pictures in the order that they occur.

a

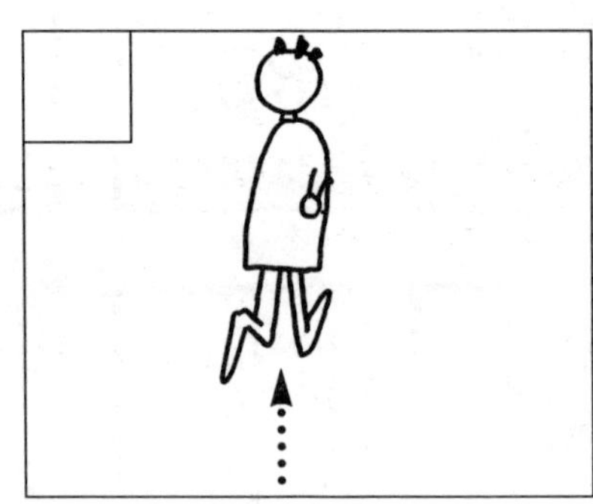

b

c

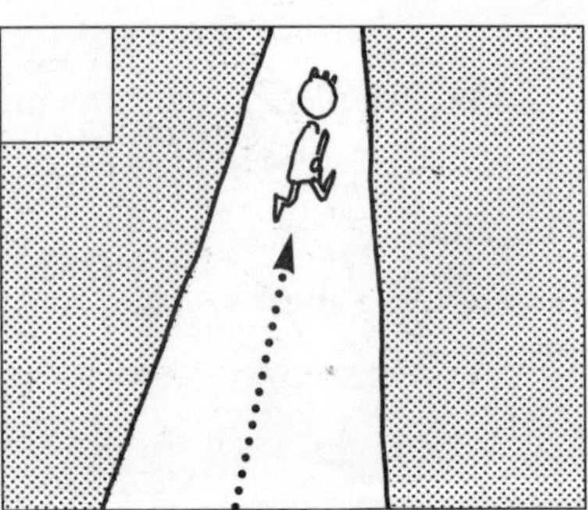

15

Complete either the beginning or end of each sentence with an initial action or a consequence. Write the last one by yourself.

たくさんあるくと、つかれます。

a 日本に行くと、＿＿＿＿＿＿＿＿＿＿＿＿＿＿＿＿＿＿＿＿。

b ＿＿＿＿＿＿＿＿＿＿＿＿＿＿＿＿＿＿＿＿と、日本語が上手になります。

c ＿＿＿＿＿＿＿＿＿＿＿＿＿＿＿＿＿＿＿＿と、海(うみ)を見ることができます。

d 冬に北海道(かいどう)に行くと、＿＿＿＿＿＿＿＿＿＿＿＿＿＿＿＿＿＿＿＿。

e ＿＿＿＿＿＿＿＿＿＿＿＿＿＿と、＿＿＿＿＿＿＿＿＿＿＿＿＿＿。

16

Your friend has given you some directions to get from the station to her house. Explain the directions to another friend by answering the questions below.

山中駅(えき)で電車をおりて、南口(ぐち)のほうに行ってください。南口の改札口(かいさつ)をとおって、外に出ると、バスとタクシーののりばがあります。私の家(うち)までは十二番(ばん)のバスにのると、いちばんかんたんで、はやいです。バスのうしろからのって、きっぷをとってください。町をとおって、図書館(と　かん)のつぎのバスていでおります。バスの前に行って、うんてんしゅさんに三百円をわたしてください。そして、バスをおりて、そのみちをまっすぐあるいて、つぎのかどを右にまがってください。すこし行くと、右側(がわ)に私の家があります。はなやのとなりにあります。家のドアはあおいですから、分(わ)かりやすいです。

単語表(たんひょう)

改札口　かいさつぐち　ticket gate

a Where do you get off the train and which way should you go?

b How do you find the right bus to take and how much will it cost?

c Did your friend tell you how to get on and off the bus?

d What do you do after alighting from the bus?

e How will you know which house it is?

17

Imagine you are an exchange student at a large school. You are not sure how to get to many of the areas around school. Ask your partner the directions to four places and s/he will respond appropriately. Then reverse roles.

Here are some suggestions for places:

ばいてん	kiosk
図書館	library
しょくいんしつ	staff room
トイレ	toilet
グラウンド	sports ground
ジム	gym
会館	hall
プール	swimming pool
校長先生のオフィス	Principal's office

Here are some handy phrases:

どうやって ～に行きますか。

右に行くと、～があります。*(If you go right, there is . . .)*

左に行くと、～が見えます。*(If you go left, . . . you can see.)*

You can also use the て form to join sentences. For example,
左にまがって、まっすぐ行ってください。

Ask your teacher if you need help with extra vocabulary.

18

Listen to the Japanese and circle or highlight the statement that best matches what you hear.

a I will go to Japan.
Please go to Japan.
I want to try to go to Japan.

b I changed trains at Tokyo station.
I will try to change trains at Tokyo station.
Please change trains at Tokyo station.

c I am studying Japanese.
I want to study Japanese.
I want to try to study Japanese.

d Please travel.
I want to travel.
I want to try travelling.

e I will turn right at that corner and go straight ahead.
I want to turn right at that corner and go straight ahead.
Please turn right at that corner and go straight ahead.

f I want to eat okonomiyaki in Japan.
I will try eating okonomiyaki in Japan.
I will eat okonomiyaki in Japan.

よっ！

19

Work with a partner to figure out the English meanings of the following sentences.

a すしを食べています。
すしを食べてください。
すしを食べてもいいですか。

b 新聞を読みます。
新聞を読みました。
新聞を読みたいです。

c おてらに行きます。
おてらを見に行きます。
おてらに行ってみたいです。

d 東京(きょう)のデパートでおみやげをさがしたいです。
東京(きょう)のデパートでおみやげをさがしてみます。
東京(きょう)のデパートでおみやげをさがしてみたいです。

e 町で買い物をしました。
町に買い物に行きましょう。
町で買い物をすることが大好きです。

f 日本のペンフレンドと電話で話しました。
日本のペンフレンドと電話で話してみたいです。
日本のペンフレンドと電話で話してみました。

20

Ask your partner the following questions. Answer using the prompts to make responses using 〜てみたいです.

a 日本で何をしてみたいですか。
I want to try to:
- eat Japanese food
- talk in Japanese
- have a Japanese bath

b 学校で何をしてみたいですか。
I want to try to:
- study hard
- do lots of homework
- join the volleyball club

c 休みに何をしてみたいですか。
I want to try to:
- go to the movies
- go travelling with a friend
- find a new penfriend

d 明日(あした)何をしてみたいですか。
I want to try to:
- make sushi
- buy a new CD
- read a Japanese comic

e 将来(しょう)、何をしてみたいですか。
I want to try to:
- go to university
- study at an Italian language school
- teach at a big and famous university

f フランスで何をしてみたいですか。
I want to try to:
- speak French everyday
- go sightseeing by myself
- read a French newspaper

21

Listen to the conversations and circle the locations they decide on.

a here / there / over there

b here / there / over there

c here / there / over there

d here / there / over there

22

Part A

In pairs, work out how to say the following conversation in Japanese.

A: Excuse me, where is the station?

B: The station? The station is over there (pointing away from both speakers).

A: Over there? How do you get there?

B: From here, turn left down this road. Go straight and then turn right at the traffic lights.

A: Over there? And turn right at the traffic lights . . .?

B: Yes. If you go straight along, the entrance to the station is on the left. It is next to the bank.

A: Yes, I understand. Thank you very much.

B: You're welcome.

Part B

Act out your dialogue in front of the class.

23

Read 見る 読む 分かる on pages 104–5 of your Student Book. In your exercise book, write a timeline of the activities Sarah did on this day.

You should include:

- where Sarah went at each stage of the day
- how Sarah got there
- Sarah's impression of the place
- what Sarah ate
- what Sarah bought

Don't forget to include points of interest on the tour.

24

Listen to 見る 聞く 分かる on page 106 of your Student Book. Note down the key points of the commentary below. Then using this information, write an itinerary for tourists covering this area of Kyoto in your exercise book. You might like to do this task in pairs.

25

Part A

In your exercise book, draw a picture representing the telephone conversation (illustrate where Sachiyo and Karen will meet and what they will do together). Don't forget to show clock faces where appropriate to indicate the different stages of the dialogue.

Part B

Read the telephone conversation and then using this information, write a note in your exercise book in Japanese for your host parents explaining your plans, detailing where you are going, who with and what time you will meet.

さちよ：もしもし。

カレン：もしもし。あっ、さちよさんですか。こんにちは。

さちよ：カレンさん、こんにちは。あのう、明日(あした)、何かよていはありますか。

カレン：いいえ、何もありませんけど。

さちよ：じゃ、いっしょに買い物に行きませんか。

カレン：ああ、いいですね。

さちよ：どこがいいですか。

カレン：渋谷(しぶや)はどうですか。

さちよ：あっ、いいですね。じゃ、デパートに行きませんか。セーターを買いたいですから。

カレン：はい、そうしましょう。渋谷(しぶや)のファッションは有(ゆう)名ですね。見てみたいです。

さちよ：人がたくさんいて、おもしろいですよ。

カレン：本屋(や)に行ってもいいですか。日本語ジャーナルというざっしがほしいですから。

さちよ：ええ、いいですよ。私も新しい辞(じ)書がいります。

カレン：じゃ、本屋(や)にも行きましょう。

さちよ：どこで会いましょうか。

カレン：そうですね。私は渋谷駅(しぶやえき)はよく分(わ)かりません。

さちよ：じゃ、渋谷(しぶや)の北口の改札(かいさつ)口はどうですか。

カレン：はい、わかりました。北口の改札(かいさつ)口ですね。

さちよ：そうです。

カレン：えきからデパートまでどのぐらいかかりますか。

さちよ：ええと、あるいて、十分ぐらいですよ。

カレン：ああ、じゃ、すぐに行けますね。

さちよ：ええ、そうですね。じゃあ、何時がいいですか。

カレン：ええと、十時はどうですか。

さちよ：はい、大丈夫(じょうぶ)です。

カレン：じゃあ、明日(あした)の十時に。

さちよ：はい、それじゃ、明日(あした)。

単語表(たんひょう)

改札口　かいさつぐち　ticket gate

26

Part A

Read the extract from a travel brochure on Shinjuku and answer the questions in English.

新宿

新宿は東京でいちばんにぎやかなところです。外国人のかんこうきゃくに人気があります。

えきの東口を出ると、大きいデパートや電気製品のみせやいろいろなレストランが見えます。新宿には、おしゃれで、すてきなレストランがあります。有名なデパートもあります。たとえば、高島屋といせたんデパートです。デートしたり、すてきなようふくを買ったりできます。スタジオアルタには、大きいテレビスクリーンがあって、とても有名です。いろいろな人がそこでまちあわせをします。わかい人がたくさん見られます。

えきの西口を出て、まっすぐ行くと、高級なホテルや会社やとちょうのビルがあって、外国人や日本人のサラリーマンがおおぜいいます。とちょうのビルにのぼると、天気のいい日には、東京のけしきが見えます。すばらしいです。

でも、新宿に行く時は、ちずを見なければなりません。大きい町ですから、すぐまよいます。一人で行くと、おもしろくないです。でも、友だちと行くと、おもしろいところです。ぜひ、新宿に来てください。たのしい時間をすごすことができます。

単語表

電気製品 でんきせいひん	electrical products
おしゃれ	stylish/beautiful
高島屋 たかしまや	Takashimaya department store
スタジオアルタ	Studio Alta
まちあわせをする	to meet
こうきゅうな	high quality
とちょう	metropolitan government
おおぜい	many/lots
まよう	to get lost

a. What kind of place is Shinjuku ?

b. What is at the east exit of Shinjuku station?

c. What is at the west exit of Shinjuku station?

d. What can you see from the top of the building?

Part B

Choose a tourist spot in your city or country and make a tourist brochure in Japanese. You might like to work with a partner. Provide a map with directions, relevant and interesting information (*i.e. historical interest spots, consulate, tourist information centre*), pictures and other information to make your brochure enticing to Japanese visitors. You might like to present your information as an electronic presentation.

Use the internet for your research!

27

Research one of the following areas:

- a place in Japan you would like to visit, what's special there?
- differences between travelling in Japan and in your own country (e.g. different styles of accommodation)
- cultural activities/festivals in different regions of Japan

おべんとうクイズ

1 Using word association, draw a line to match the logical pairs.

電車	左
いなか	かど
右	おてら
こうさてん	町
神社(じんじゃ)	地下鉄(ちかてつ)

2 Match the words with their meanings.

修学旅行(しゅうがくりょこう) •	• 飛行機(ひこうき)のきっぷ
日程(にってい) •	• 外(そと)で食べること
見物 •	• いろいろなところを見ること
外食(がいしょく) •	• 学校で旅(りょ)行すること
こうくうけん •	• 毎日のよてい

3 Write the number of the strokes of each kanji.

a 町 ☐

b 東 ☐

c 西 ☐

d 南 ☐

e 北 ☐

f 食べ物 ☐☐

g 飲み物 ☐☐

4 What do the following directions mean in English?

a このみちをまっすぐ行ってください。

b つぎのかどを右にまがってください。

c 左にまがると、はしが見えます。そのはしをわたってください。

5 The phrases in the box are the endings to the following sentences. Work out which phrase is the correct ending and then join the sentences using ～と. Write the meaning underneath in English.

> えきが見えます。
> 上手になります。
> さくらが見えます。

a 春になります。

b まっすぐ行きます。

c たくさんれんしゅうします。

Use the plain *(dictionary)* form before ～と.

6 Look at the timetable and work out how long it takes to get to the following places from Tokyo by plane.

東京(きょう)から札幌(さっぽろ)まで飛(ひ)行機(き)で行くと、一時間半かかります。

a 函館 ______

b 大阪 ______

c 広島 ______

d 松山 ______

東京(とうきょう)	→	札幌(さっぽろ)
05.50		07.20
09.30		11.00
東京(とうきょう)	→	函館(はこだて)
12.30		13.50
17.05		18.25
10.15		11.35
東京(とうきょう)	→	大阪(おおさか)
07.45		09.00
15.00		16.15
20.35		21.50
東京(とうきょう)	→	広島(ひろしま)
06.55		08.10
18.10		19.25
東京(とうきょう)	→	松山(まつやま)
06.55		08.15
17.50		19.10

7 How do you say these in Japanese?

a It takes one hour from Tokyo to Sapporo by plane.

b It takes about two hours from Kyoto to Hiroshima by bullet train.

c It takes thirty minutes from Shinjuku to Ginza on the subway.

d It takes about eight hours from Sydney to Tokyo by plane.

8 Read the letter about Anne's forthcoming travels to Japan and answer the questions in English.

みずほさんへ

　こんにちは。お元気ですか。私も元気です。日本の天気はどうですか。今、オーストラリアはとてもさむいです。

　私は来月の十五日に、学校の日本ツアーに行きます。とてもたのしみです。一週間、山形県(がたけん)でホームステイをします。きれいないなかの町です。日本のりょうりが大好きです。とくに、毎日おいしいさしみとすしを食べたいです。そして、日本のテレビも見てみたいです。ホームステイのあとで、みんなですこしかんこうができます。東京(きょう)と日光(こう)に行ってみたいです。

　ところで、東京(きょう)でみずほさんに会えますか。いっしょにかんこうや買い物をしませんか。おへんじをたのしみにしています。からだに気をつけてください。さようなら。

8月2日

アンより

単語表(たんひょう)

ところで by the way

a When does Anne go to Japan?

b What does Anne want to do most in Japan?

c Where does she want to go?

9 Your Japanese friend has left a message on your answering machine. Before you call him back, prepare what you will say. You plan to meet him on Tuesday at 9.30 at his hotel. You will show him around Perth and then have lunch at Fremantle. You will go by boat to Fremantle and will be back at the hotel around 5pm.

もしもし。チェルシーさんですか。よしひでです。ぼくは来週の月曜日にパースにつきます。ぼくにパースをあんないしてくれませんか。ぼくのホテルの名前はシービューです。ホテルの電話番号(ばんごう)は9734−5111です。じゃね、さようなら。お電話をまっています。

7 ちきゅうにやさしく

1

Answer the following questions in English.

a. How do you contribute to recycling programs and enviromental conservation?

b. Why do you think different countries have different environmental conservation priorities?

c. Are there any environmental issues you think need addressing in your country. If yes, please explain.

d. What do you think the main environmental issues are in a country like Japan?

2

Refer to the Unit 7 漢字の書き方 on page 143 for the stroke order practice of the kanji introduced in this unit. There are also reading and writing exercises and a game or puzzle for you to practise the new kanji.

3

Sort the following items according to whether they are もえるごみ or もえないごみ by completing the table below.

あきかん	テレビ	タイル	タイヤ
ビニールぶくろ	ペットボトル	オイル	新聞
かみ	まんが	自転車	ざっし

もえるごみ	もえないごみ

4

You will be asked to listen and/or read the 会話 in the Student Book on pages 113–15 and then read this summary. Note the main points from the summary below and then compare this information with the Student Book 会話. Underline any parts in the summary that don't match the Student Book and write the correct information underneath.

　ようへいくんは先週リサイクルのレポートを書かなければなりませんでした。でも、ようへいくんはあんまりしらべることができなかったと言いました。インターネットや本やざっしをつかって、べんきょうしました。でも、ぜんぜんじょうほうがありませんでしたから、書くことができませんでした。ようへいくんは明日(あした)までに、レポートを書かなければなりません。だから、今プリントアウトをしてみています。綾(あや)子さんはかみがリサイクルできると言いました。リサイクルしないと、もったいないと思っています。

　ようへいくんはゆめを見ました。ゆめの中でいろいろなおもしろい物を見ました。ペットボトルが木になったり、木やビニールぶくろがオイルになったり、グラスが金属(きんぞく)になったりしました。ようへいくんはびっくりしました。このゆめを見たあとで、ようへいくんはかみをリサイクルしたいと言いました。

5

Tick the preference you hear.

- **a** 海　　プール
- **b** くろい　　あかい
- **c** 東京(きょう)タワー　　とちょうのビル
- **d** 高島屋(しまや)　　西武(ぶ)
- **e** バイオリン　　ギター

6

With a partner, use the pictures to practise asking preferences and responding.

〜さんは、〜と〜とでは、どちらのほうが（いい）ですか。

〜のほうが（いい）です。

a

c

b

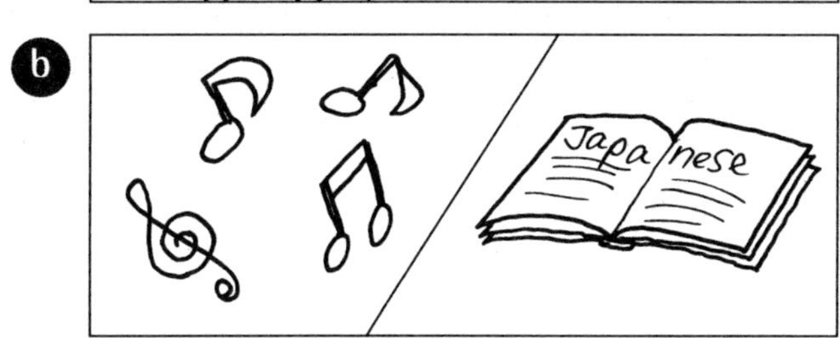

d

7

Survey five people in your class to find out their preferences. Use the following questions and record your results in the table.

べんきょうとスポーツとでは、どちらのほうが好きですか。

電車と車とでは、どちらのほうがいいですか。

夏と冬とでは、どちらのほうが好きですか。

ポップスとクラシックとでは、どちらのほうがいいですか。

日本語と数学（すう）とでは、どちらのほうがむずかしいですか。

名前					
べんきょう / スポーツ					
電車 / 車					
夏 / 冬					
ポップス / クラシック					
日本語 / 数学（すう）					

8

Ken is interviewing Tina about recycling. Read the interview and answer the questions.

けん: ティナさんの国では、かんきょうのためにどんなことをしていますか。
ティナ: そうですね。いろいろな物をリサイクルしたり、水や電気をせつやくしたりしています。
けん： そうですか。何をリサイクルしていますか。
ティナ: いろいろな物をリサイクルしています。たとえば、かみやびんやプラスチックなどです。
けん: 家でごみを分(わ)けますか。
ティナ: はい、分(わ)けますよ。
けん: ああ、そうですか。どうやって、分(わ)けますか。
ティナ: まず、もえるごみともえないごみに分(わ)けます。
けん: ああ、それは、日本とおなじですね。
ティナ: そうですか。それから、びんとかんとプラスチックと電池(ち)をそれぞれべつべつに分(わ)けます。
けん: もえるごみともえないごみとでは、どちらのほうがおおいですか。
ティナ: そうですね。もえないごみのほうがおおいと思います。
けん: どうしてですか。
ティナ: 生ごみは「コンポスター」をつかって、家でリサイクルできるからです。だから、もえるごみがすくなくなります。
けん: そうですか。ほかに、かんきょうもんだいについて、何かしていますか。
ティナ: そうですね。家や学校で電気や水をせつやくしています。一人一人のどりょくが大切(せつ)だと思います。
けん: ぼくも、そうだと思います。
ティナ: 車やバスはかんきょうにわるいですから、私はよく、自転(てん)車で町や友だちの家に行きます。時々、リサイクリングもしますから、ぜんぜん病(びょう)気になりません。
けん: すばらしいですね。「かんきょうにやさしく」は、けんこうにもいいんですね。

日本語でこたえてください。

- **a** ティナさんの国では、何をリサイクルしますか。
- **b** 家で、どうやってごみを分(わ)けますか。
- **c** もえるごみともえないごみとでは、どちらのほうがおおいですか。

単語表(たんごひょう)

かんきょうのために	for the *(sake of)* the environment
せつやくする	to conserve/save
一人一人	everyone/every person
どりょく	effort
病気になる びょうきになる	to become sick
けんこう	*(one's)* health

9

With a partner, brainstorm the ます form and the plain past form of these verbs. The steps below might help you.

- **a** to write ________( ) ________
- **b** to read ________( ) ________
- **c** to throw out ________( ) ________
- **d** to see/watch ________( ) ________
- **e** to think ________( ) ________
- **f** to do/play ________( ) ________
- **g** to come ________( ) ________
- **h** to go ________( ) ________
- **i** to look up ________( ) ________
- **j** to speak/talk ________( ) ________

1 Write the ます form for each verb.
2 Categorise the verb as Group 1, 2 or Irregular (I) and record it in the bracket.
3 Work out the て form. Then change the て to た and record it in the space.

10

What do the following people do in their time off? Listen to the recording and answer in point form in English according to what you hear.

a Yoshi ______________________________

____

b Tomoko ______________________________

____

c Yuri ______________________________

____

d Mami ______________________________

____

e Chiho ______________________________

____

11

Complete the chart.

English	Plain (dictionary) form	て form	～たり
to eat	食べる	食べて	食べたり
	読む		
			書いたり
to buy			
		あらって	
			あそんだり
to throw out			
	する		

12

Fill in the blanks with appropriate activities using the ～たり～たり pattern.

- **a** ひまな時、友だちと＿＿＿＿＿＿＿＿、＿＿＿＿＿＿＿＿します。
- **b** 学校で、＿＿＿＿＿＿＿＿、＿＿＿＿＿＿＿＿しました。
- **c** 日本に行くと、＿＿＿＿＿＿＿＿、＿＿＿＿＿＿＿＿できます。
- **d** 春休みに、＿＿＿＿＿＿＿＿、＿＿＿＿＿＿＿＿したいです。

13

In your exercise book, respond to the question by writing some sentences using the て form and some using the ～たり ～たり pattern. Study the example before you begin.

月曜日に、何をしますか。

月曜日は、学校に行って、友だちとバスケットボールをして、八時半に英語のじゅうぎょうに出ます。

月曜日は、コンピューターゲームをしたり、先生と話したり、スポーツをしたりします。

Use the て form for actions you always do. List them in the order you do them.

Use the たり form for actions you sometimes do or a list of actions not necessarily done in a particular order.

14

Read the article written by the Yamanokawa National Park Ranger.

山の川国立公園パークレーンジャーからのメッセージ

ハイキング

今年は秋のけしきがとてもきれいですから、たくさんの人がハイキングをすると思います。かならず、小道をあるいてください。それから、小道のよこの植物にさわったり、とったりしてはだめです。ピクニックのあとでごみをもってかえらなければなりません。みなさん、山の川国立公園でのハイキングをたのしんでください。

キャンプ

みなさんはキャンプをするのとホテルにとまるのとでは、どちらのほうがおもしろいと思いますか。私はキャンプのほうがおもしろいと思います。みんなであるいたり、自然をたのしんだり、きれいなけしきを見たりしましょう。キャンプでは、バーベキューをすることもできます。もちろん、ごみはもってかえりましょう。

やせい動物

やせい動物に食べ物をやってはだめです。ふとったり、病気になったりするからです。

私たちの食べ物は私たちだけで食べましょう。やせい動物は自然の食べ物だけ食べなければなりません。

Part A

Jot down the main points of the article in your exercise book. With a partner or in a small group, discuss the main points and your opinions on these issues.

Part B

Discuss your ideas as a class. Are there other issues that should be considered when visiting a National Park?

単語表

小道 こみち	small paths/walking trails
やせい動物 やせいどうぶつ	wild/native animals
食べ物をやる	to give food *(to animals)*

15

Read the statements before you listen to the recording and as you listen, circle the correct meaning.

test?

a
- I think I want to study Japanese.
- I think that Japanese study is interesting.
- They say that the study of Japanese is interesting.

b
- I think that pet bottles are better than cans.
- I think that glass bottles are better than pet bottles.
- I think that pet bottles are better than glass bottles.

c
- In my summer holidays, I like listening to music and telephoning my friends.
- In my spare time, I like playing music and mucking around with my friends.
- In my summer holidays, I like listening to music and going to the beach with my friends.

d
- I said there is a test next month.
- I think there is a test next month.
- I think there is a test next week.

There are fun games you can play using these patterns. Ask your teacher for ideas.

e
- I think my older sister likes judo better than kendo.
- I think my older brother likes kendo better than judo.
- I think my older brother likes judo better than kendo.

16

Give the English equivalent under each comment.

a 私はリサイクルはとても大事(だいじ)だと思います。せかい中で、リサイクルしなければなりませんね。

____

____

b ぼくはこれから、もっとリサイクルをしたいと思います。

____

c 私は自然(ぜん)が大好きだから、ネパールを旅(りょ)行したいと思います。

____

d いつもリサイクルすることは大変(へん)ですが、大切(たいせつ)だと思います。

____

e ぼくはリサイクルは、あんまりむずかしくないと思います。

____

17

Unjumble and rewrite the following sentences according to the English meaning.

a ごみ　すてて　と　に　を　はだめです。　海　川

____

You must not throw rubbish into seas and rivers etc.

b けした　を　は　父　ヒーター　と言いました。

____

My father said that he turned the heater off.

c は　かんきょうもんだい　おもしろい　は　の　私　と思います。　とても　べんきょう

____

____

I think that the study of environmental issues is very interesting.

d リサイクルのかみ　新しいかみ　いい　のほうが　と思います。　より　は　私

____

____

I think that recycled paper is better than unused paper.

e 海　に　友だち　行ったり　と思います。サッカー　と　を　したり　明日　したい

____

____

Tomorrow I think I want to go the beach and play soccer with my friend.

18

Listen to the interviews about recycling to complete the responses in English.

a (i) The lady thinks that recycling is very

______________________________.

(ii) She collects *(choose three alternatives)*
- paper
- cans
- bottles
- vegetable and garden rubbish

b (i) The student recycles
(choose three alternatives)
- paper
- bottles
- cans
- plastic

c (i) Do they recycle at this company?

____

(ii) The company spokesperson believes that ______________________________ forklifts are better for the environment than ______________________________ forklifts.

d **(i)** What does this person recycle in their country? (Give three examples.)____________________

____

(ii) What else do they say about companies and how do they feel about this?____________________

____

19

Read the article from a Japanese recycling advisor. Put the information into point form and then make a picture book with simple explanations for a younger learner of Japanese.

できることから一歩(いっぽ)ずつ、ストップちきゅうおんだんか

今月の新聞のテーマは「リサイクルをして、ちきゅうにやさしくしましょう」です。ちきゅうおんだんかが大きいもんだいになっています。このちきゅうおんだんかをとめなければなりません。エネスタイル（エネルギーライフスタイル）をかえましょう。

だいどころ

- れいぞうこに物をたくさん入れてはだめです。
- 食器(しょっき)あらいの時は、水をせつやくしてください。

おふろの入り方(かた)をかえる

- シャワーの水をたくさんつかってはだめです。
- おふろは、前の人のあとにすぐ入ってください。

水のつかいかたをかえる

- はをみがく時は、コップをつかいましょう。
- 毎日より、一回(いっかい)でたくさんのふくをあらいましょう。
- リサイクルのせっけんをつかいましょう。

リビングの生活(かつ)をかえる

- 一晩中(ひとばんじゅう)エアコンをつかってはだめです。
- テレビをながい時間見てはだめです。電気をせつやくしましょう。

カーライフをかえる

- バケツに水を入れて、車をあらってください。ホースよりバケツのほうがいいです。
- 電車をつかってください。あるいてください。

単語表(たんひょう)

せつやくする	to conserve
一晩中 ひとばんじゅう	all night
バケツ	bucket
ホース	hose

Try out your book with some young learners at your school.

20

Discuss some or all of the following topics in pairs or small groups. Choose a spokesperson to report some of your views to the class. Try to find information relating to Japan as well as your own country. Before you start your discussion, make some notes in point form *(English or Japanese)* in your exercise book.

- **paper recycling**
- **sorting household rubbish**
- **saving water**
- **walking or riding a bike instead of using the car**

Try to use the following question and answer to structure your discussion.

〜さんは、〜についてどう思いますか。

私／ぼくは〜は〜と思います。／私は〜より〜のほうが〜と思います。

21

Listen to the quotes given to complete the sentences in English.

a Your friend said ____________________

b Ms Yamaguchi said ____________________

c Chris said ____________________

d The teacher said ____________________

22

Rewrite these sentences so that the person in the brackets has said them and then check you know the English meaning.

家でリサイクルしています。(母)

母は家でリサイクルしていると言いました。

a パーティーに行きたいです。(エミリー)

____

b 明日(あした)かんじのテストがあります。(先生)

____

c サッカーのれんしゅうに行けません。(友だち)

____

d このみせでリサイクルのぶんぼうぐがかえます。(安子)

____

e ペットボトルからカーペットがつくれます。(父)

____

23

Here is an entry for a forthcoming poster competition.

Think about how you will make your poster eye-catching. What language and illustrations will you use?

ポスターコンクール!

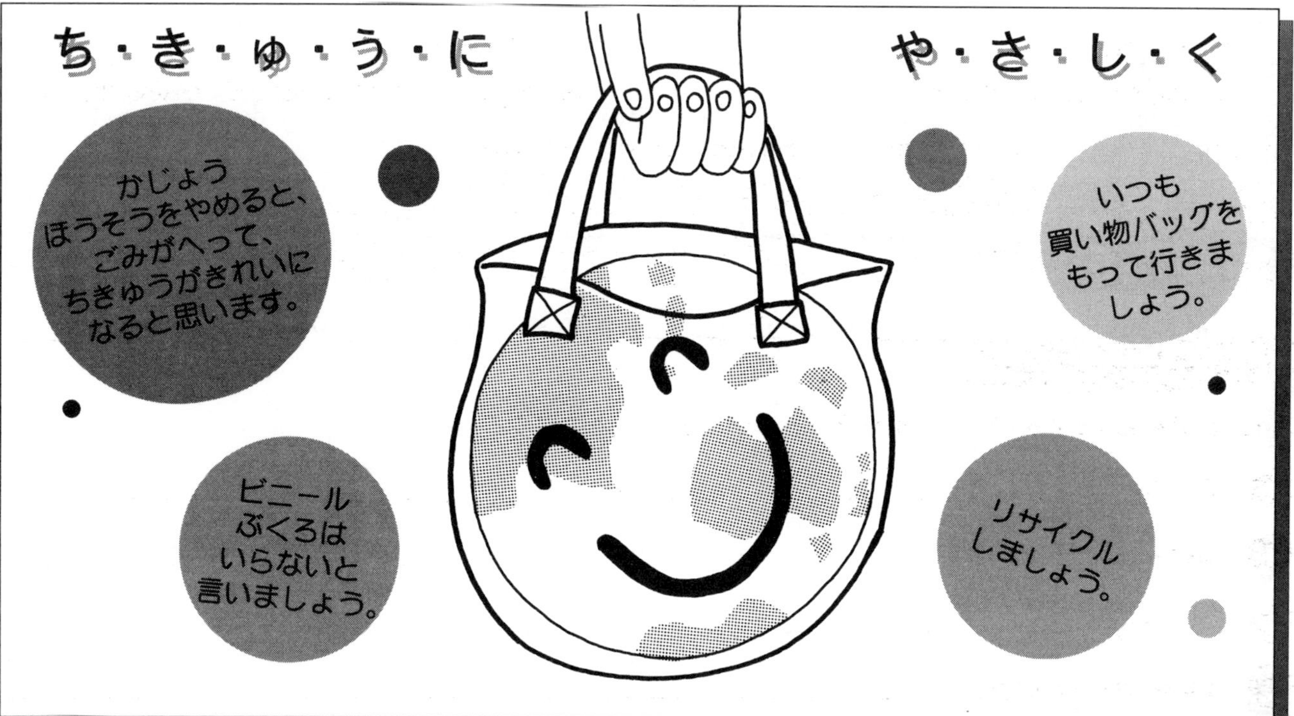

Part A

With a partner, answer the questions in English.

a What is this poster about?

b What do you think of the issues raised?

Part B

Make your own poster in Japanese to raise awareness about an environmental issue.

単語表(たんごひょう)

コンクール	competition
かじょうほうそう	excess wrapping
へる	to decrease

24

Listen to Hiro telling Chieko about his English class yesterday. Using the list of names given, indicate who said each of the statements in class. The statements are not in the order you will hear them, so read through them before you start.

名前:	けい子	しんじ	ともみ	先生	ひろ

Name	Statement
ひろ	じゅぎょうでごみについて話しました。
	えきにいろいろなごみばこがあります。
	ちきゅうにやさしくしなければなりません。
	リサイクルはむずかしくないです。
	ペットボトルやかみなどをリサイクルすることができます。

7

百五

25

Part A

Read 見る 読む 分(わ)かる on page 123 of your Student Book. Write down the main points in your exercise book and then summarise it for a short oral presentation in Japanese.

Part B

Read the short story on page 124 of your Student Book. Two people are mentioned. Who do you support and why? Discuss your reasons in small groups. You might also be able to have a class discussion on this issue.

26

Read through these questions first, and then listen to 見る 聞く 分(わ)かる on page 126 of your Student Book. Answer the questions about it in Japanese.

a ナターシャさんの友だちの由美子(ゆみ)さんは何がおいしいと言いましたか。

____

b ようへいくんはやきそばと天(てん)ぷらうどんとでは、どちらのほうがおいしいと思いましたか。

____

c ウエイターは何と言いましたか。

____

d ナターシャさんはさいごに何と言いましたか。

____

e わりばしとおはしとでは、どちらのほうがいいと思いますか。

____

27

In groups of four or five people, discuss **one** of the following topics and then give a class presentation about it in Japanese.

- Yard duty（そうじとうばん）should be compulsory
- All students should collect rubbish at school.
- There should be compulsory recycling of paper and cans at school.
- More homes should recycle.

Some handy phrases:
～しないと、～です。
～すると、～です／できます。
～からです。
～から～と思います。

You could also have a class debate.

First decide on your group's viewpoint. It doesn't matter if you disagree, so long as you are able to give a reason for your viewpoint. Each person should prepare at least two or three sentences giving their own views on the topic. You may like to appoint a spokesperson for the introduction and conclusion. Study the example below before you begin.

Introduction: 学生のそうじとうばんについて話しました。みなさんは、どう思いますか。

Conclusion: 私たちは、そうじとうばんは大切（せつ）だと思います。

28

Read the email from Helen's penpal in Japan. Imagine you are Helen and write a short reply to Yukiko in Japanese in your exercise book to respond to her questions.

ヘレンさん、

こんにちは。お元気ですか。私も家族（ぞく）も元気です。オーストラリアの天気はどうですか。日本はすこしさむいです。もうすぐ冬ですね。

今、学校でかんきょうについてのレポートを書いています。むずかしいですが、おもしろいです。私のクラスはいろいろな国のことをしらべています。先生は外国からたくさん学ぶことができると言いました。私にはペンフレンドのヘレンさんがいますから、オーストラリアをしらべたいと思います。英語が下手ですから、日本語でしつもんをしてもいいですか。おねがいします。

- かんきょうほごについてどう思いますか。
- オーストラリア人は何をリサイクルしますか。
- ヘレンさんの学校には、かんきょうクラブがありますか。
- そのクラブはどんなかつどうをしますか。ヘレンさんは入っていますか。
- ヘレンさんの学校には、リサイクルのプログラムがありますか。
- 学校では、何がリサイクルできますか。
- どんなオーストラリアの動（どう）物をほごしなければなりませんか。
- ヘレンさんの家では何をリサイクルしていますか。

しつもんがたくさんあって、すみません。では、おからだに気をつけてください。

おへんじをたのしみにしています。

２０００年１１月１９日

雪子より

単語表（たんひょう）

学ぶ まなぶ	to learn
ほご（する）	protection *(to protect)*
かんきょうクラブ	Environmental club

29

Write a letter to Masako who is an exchange student from Nagasaki. She is coming to stay with your family for two weeks. Choose four of the following topics to write about in detail. For each paragraph, write three or four sentences.

- **family**
- **weather**
- **hobbies**
- **sport**
- **sightseeing**
- **hometown**
- **part-time work**
- **school**
- **environmental issues**

Start by writing a plan *(English or Japanese)* using the space below. Try to use a range of grammar patterns. Go back through your notes or your Student Book to include phrases you have studied. However, only use them if they relate to what you are saying. Ask your teacher for the assessment criteria.

Introduction	
Main theme	**Vocabulary/grammar patterns**
Topic 1: **Topic 2:** **Topic 3:** **Topic 4:**	
Concluding remarks	

Don't try to use too many new words. Although it is good to use your dictionary for some new words, try to limit your writing to words you already know.

If you are using げんこうようし revise the writing rules.

30

Part A

In pairs or in small groups, choose **Part A** or **Part B** to complete **one** of the topics below to research and present your findings to the class.

- recycling methods in Japan
- gift wrapping in Japan
- household recycling in Japan
- attitudes to recycling among young Japanese people
- Japan's environment protection strategies

You may be able to do this over the internet using email.

Part B

Interview a Japanese person about their views on recycling.

おべんとうクイズ

1 Write these verbs in the plain form and the たり form and then check you know their meanings in English.

a すてます ______

b リサイクルします ______

c しらべます ______

d あらいます ______

e もえます ______

2 Write the number of the description for each of the following words.

a せかい ☐

b もえるごみ ☐

c ゆめ ☐

d ペットボトル ☐

e わりばし ☐

f ごみ ☐

g ゆめのしま ☐

1 かみや木や生ごみです。すてることができません。

2 ねている時に見ます。本当(とう)じゃないです。

3 ジュースが入っていません。ぜんぶジュースを飲みました。

4 しまです。ごみでつくりました。

5 私たちはここに住んでいます。

6 きたないものです。いりません。

7 木でつくりました。一回(かい)だけつかいます。

3 Write the kanji readings.

a 川（　）と海（　）をきれいにしましょう。

b この国（　）も外国（　）もリサイクルをしなければなりません。

c 海外（　）に日本（　）の会社（　）がたくさんあります。

d あねの友（　）だちは社会（　）の先生（　）です。

4 How well do you know the stroke order of the new kanji? Show the stroke order below.

a 川 ______

b 海 ______

______

c 国 ______

______

d 外 ______

e 友 ______

f 思 ______

______

g 社 ______

5 Divide these kanji into three categories of related meaning.

人	海	思	母	国
山	行	友	読	父
言	川	見	私	町

Category 1	Category 2	Category 3

6 With a partner, take it in turns to read aloud these questions and answer them.

a 何をリサイクルしますか。

b この国のごみのもんだいがありますか。

c 学校でかんきょうやリサイクルについてべんきょうをしましたか。どんなことをべんきょうしましたか。

d 母は家のごみを分(わ)けなければならないと言いました。あなたの家ではどうしますか。

7 Sort the phrases into three sentences according to the English meanings below.

学校のあとで、　　　海でおよいだり
夏休みに　　　　　　したいと思います。
新しいかみとでは、　川でつりをしたり、
どちらのほうが　　　リサイクルのかみと
することがたのしいです。
友だちと買い物をしたり
ミスタードーナツに行ったり
ちきゅうにやさしいと思いますか。

a In the summer holidays, I want to swim at the beach and go fishing at the river.
b After school, it is fun to go shopping with my friends and going to Mister Donuts.
c Which do you think is better for the environment, recycled paper or new paper?

8 Read Mark's letter and answer the questions in English.

山口先生、日本語のクラスのみなさんへ、
　こんにちは。みなさんはお元気ですか。
ぼくはもう二か月日本にいます。
しんじられません。
　今、オーストラリアの天気はどうですか。
日本はまだとてもむしあつくて、大変(へん)です。
　日本人の生活(かつ)について、たくさん
べんきょうしています。きょうみぶかくて、
おもしろいです。ぼくは東京(きょう)のちかくに
住んでいます。とても人がおおいですから、
ごみは大変(へん)なもんだいで、リサイクルを
しなければなりません。きびしいです。
とてもびっくりしました。
　まず、ごみは家でもえるごみともえない
ごみに分(わ)けれなければなりません。そして、
新聞などはまとめて、しばらなければ
なりません。それから、ごみを出す日が
ちがいます。オーストラリアでは、ごみを
ぜんぶおなじ日に出しますね。日本では、
家のちかくのごみおきばまでもっていきます。
　それに、大きいごみを出す時は、お金を
はらわなければなりません。たとえば、
テレビは五百円で、自転(てん)車は二百五十円
です。だから、物をすてる時は、
よくかんがえなければなりません。
　私は毎日、電車で学校に行きます。
どこにもリサイクルようのごみばこが
たくさんあります。えきや、学校にも
あります。かんとびんとかみを分(わ)けて
すてることができます。すごいです。
　日本人は物をたくさん買いますが、
リサイクルもたくさんしています。
　では、みなさんもいろいろリサイクル
してみてください。また手紙(がみ)を書きます。
２００２年９月１１日
マークより

単語表(たんごひょう)
ごみおきば　rubbish disposal area
どこにも　everywhere

a What are Mark's attitudes about recycling in the home?

____

b What is the procedure for disposing of large pieces of rubbish?

____

c What does he see on his way to school that surprises him?

____

d What final comment does he make about Japan?

____

9 Write a report about what recycling you do in your home or at school. Use the new grammar from this unit as well as the grammar structures from earlier units. The following questions may assist you.

- 家か学校でリサイクルしますか。
- 何をリサイクルしますか。
- だれがリサイクルしますか。
- 家族(ぞく)も友だちもしますか。
- リサイクルすると、何がいいと思いますか。
- 本当(とう)にかんきょうにやさしいと思いますか。
- どうしてそう思いますか。
- 先生／家族(ぞく)の人はリサイクルについて何と言いましたか。

8 わらって！ HEY! HEY!

1

This unit presents a Japanese style variety show. List the four segments that make up the show and give a brief summary in English.

1 ______________________________

2 ______________________________

3 ______________________________

4 ______________________________

2

Search for the words or phrases in the puzzle. They can be found running horizontally *(right to left)*, diagonally downwards, or vertically *(up or down)*. The remaining letters will complete the message.

invention	Japanese style mattress	Chihuahua	by all means	to consult	steps
to put	a worry	problem	special	solar battery	around
bottle	point	if it rains	when it rains	scores	tube
rainwater	dangerous	in fact	to receive	to laugh	to call
the whole time		to flow	comfortable	compere	lastly
panel					well/now

お	じ	司(し)	会	者(しゃ)	ぜ	な	が	れ	る
は	つ	め	い	ひ	め	や	で	さ	か
チ	は	つ	雨	の	時	み	て	と	い
ワ	ま	い	が	水	び	う	よ	あ	て
ワ	わ	だ	ふ	と	ん	お	ぶ	さ	き
と	り	ん	っ	く	太(たい)	な	く	い	な
く	ず	も	た	て	い	陽(よう)	ご	ご	ん
べ	ざ	っ	ら	ん	い	わ	電	に	だ
つ	か	い	と	う	し	ゃ	ら	池(ち)	い
な	そ	う	だ	ん	す	る	ま	う	か

Message:

___ ___ ___ ___ ___

___ ___ ___ ___ す。

3

You will be asked to listen and/or read わらって！HEY! HEY!. Indicate whether the statements below are true or false using ○（まる） or ×（ばつ）.

- a ☐ There are four celebrities on the panel for わらって！HEY! HEY!
- b ☐ Yasuko Ito recently bought a fire engine.
- c ☐ This week's guest on the 「みんな友だち」segment is called Akemi and she is twenty-two years old.
- d ☐ Akemi's favourite subject is computing and she wants to become a computer programmer.
- e ☐ Akemi hasn't met any friends through the internet who can speak Japanese.
- f ☐ Akemi spends about fifty hours a week on the internet.
- g ☐ Her Canadian friend Rene currently lives in Toronto, but will come over for the show next week.
- h ☐ Natsuko Yamamoto used to sleep on a futon.
- i ☐ Natsuko's pet is a cheetah and she bought a new bunk bed for it.
- j ☐ The panel considered Natsuko's problem, but solved it by giving her a trampoline.
- k ☐ Terumi Takeuchi sang a funny song.
- l ☐ Goro Takayama's invention could be worn in the rain.
- m ☐ Kyoko Fujisato's invention could not be worn in the rain.
- n ☐ Goro's invention won the prize to Disneyland.
- o ☐ If you want to be in the audience for the Inventor's Corner segment you must ring after 10:30 on Thursday 28th November.

4

You are a guest in the みんな友だち segment on this week's program. Note down your answers to the compere's questions and then rehearse with a partner.

お名前は何ですか。 ______________________

おいくつですか。 ______________________

学校で何をべんきょうしていますか。 ______________________

いちばん好きなかもくは何ですか。 ______________________

アルバイトをしていますか。 ______________________

どんなしごとですか。 ______________________

スポーツチームに入っていますか。 ______________________

どんなスポーツをしますか。 ______________________

しゅみは何ですか。 ______________________

だれとしますか。 ______________________

いつしますか。 ______________________

将(しょう)来、何になりたいですか。 ______________________

5

Complete the following script using appropriate words or phrases.

司会者: こんにちは。＿＿＿＿＿＿＿＿＿＿スペシャルです。みなさん、お元気ですか。今日のかいとうしゃは、＿＿＿＿人です。高村みどりさん、岩下＿＿＿＿＿さん、山口＿＿＿＿＿さんです。

かいとうしゃ: こんにちは。＿＿＿＿＿＿＿＿＿＿。

司会者: みどりさん、さいきん、子犬を買ったそうですね。どんないぬですか。

みどり: ＿＿＿＿＿＿＿、＿＿＿＿＿＿＿いぬです。でも、いぬはいつもおなかがすいていますよ。

司会者: ペコペコですか。

みどり: ええ、きのう、＿＿＿＿＿＿＿＿を九つ食べました！

司会者: ほんとう！！！

6

Think about an invention you could present in the はつめいじっけんしつ segment. Illustrate your invention and label it in Japanese. Then write at least three sentences in Japanese to describe your invention using adjectives. Give a brief explanation of who could use it and when they could use it.

Look up CHINDOGU or www.chindogu.com on the internet for unusual Japanese inventions or refer to *101 Unuseless Japanese Inventions. The Art of Chindogu* by Kenji Kawakami (W.W. Norton & Company).

7

Develop an advertisement that promotes your favourite program or one that you have made up yourself. Include visual information and voice overs to say what the show is like, when it's on, and how to become a member of the audience. Refer to your Student Book on page 139 for ideas.

8

Working in a group, choose a Japanese song you have already learnt, or ask your teacher for the words to a new Japanese song, or write your own song in Japanese. Sing the song to your class, paying attention to pronunciation and accuracy. One of the group members might like to develop a script to introduce the song and to close the segment. Refer to page 136 in your Student Book for ideas.

You can also present your song as a solo.

9

This is a segment which is often featured in a variety show. Here, a reporter visits a different restaurant each week and gives a live report back to the studio audience. Listen to Kaori Tokunaga's report about this week's restaurant and answer the questions in English in your exercise book.

司会者(しかいしゃ): りょうりのレポーターのとくながかおりさんから、つぎのレポートをもらっています。とくながさん、今晩(こんばん)はどんなりょうりですか。

とくなが: 今晩(こんばん)は、すしを食べてみたいですね。このあたりには、すしやがたくさんありますが、このすしやはちょっとかわっています。新しいタイプのレストランで、「すしーGO-ROUND」と言います。このすしやでは、ベルト・コンベアーがカウンターのまわりをまわっています。コンベアの上に、いろいろなすしのおさらがのっていて、好きなすしのおさらをとるんです。ふとまきや、にぎりずしなどがありますね。このすしはカリフォルニアロールです。このカリフォルニアロールを食べてみましょう。. . . ああ、おいしいですね。すしのさらのいろはあかや、あおや、しろなど、いろいろあります。あかいさらのすしは、二百五十円、しろいさらは三百円で、一つ一つは高くないですよ。友だちと行くと、おもしろいと思います。新宿駅(しんじゅくえき)から銀行(ぎんこう)が見えますから、その銀行(ぎんこう)にむかって、まっすぐ行って、つぎのかどを左にまがってください。大きいかんばんがありますから、分(わ)かりやすいですよ。

司会者(しかいしゃ): とくながさん、どうもありがとうございました。じゃまた、来週。

とくなが: はい、ありがとうございました。

単語表(たんごひょう)

このあたり	around here
かわっている	to be unusual
おさら	plate/dish
一つ一つ	one by one
むかう	to face towards
かんばん	sign/billboard
分(わ)かりやすい	easy to understand

- **a** What is the name of the restaurant and what kind of restaurant is it?
- **b** What three types of sushi are available?
- **c** Which one does Kaori choose and how does she describe it?
- **d** How is the bill calculated in this restaurant? Give an example.
- **e** How do you get to the restaurant from Shinjuku Station?

10

Read the following letter from a viewer and in your exercise book, write a possible solution in Japanese for the わらって！HEY!HEY! panel to provide. Your reply can be a return letter, or a manga for the panel (script with illustrations). Before you begin, with a partner, discuss the issue and your possible solution. Refer to pages134–5 in your Student Book for ideas.

わらって！HEY! HEY! かいとうしゃのみなさまへ、

私は文子(ふみこ)で、十五才(さい)です。さいきん、りょうしんがとても高いソファーを買いました。きのう、友だちのけいすけくんが私の家にしゅくだいをしに来ました。べんきょうをしたり、コーラを飲んだり、テレビを見たりしました。たのしかったです。私はけいすけくんが大好きです。

けいすけくんがかえる時に、私にキスをしてくれました。その時、コーラのびんをひっくりかえしました。コーラをぜんぶ飲んでいませんでしたから、新しいソファーがよごれました。今、私はそのしみの上に、ざぶとんをおいてかくしています。だから、りょうしんはまだそのしみを見ていません。

どうしたらいいですか。このもんだいをかいけつしてください。

よろしくおねがいします。

２００１年１０月２７日

さたけ文子(ふみこ)より

単語表(たんごひょう)

りょうしん	parents
かえる時に	when *(he)* left
～てくれる	do me the favour of .../to me
ひっくりかえす	*(I)* tip over
よごれる	to be stained
しみ	stain
ざぶとん	cushion
かくす	to hide

Remember in this segment of the show, prizes are given away to solve the problems raised.

8

Mock Test

/250

This test is made up of five sections: Kanji, Listening, Speaking, Reading and Writing. Each section totals 50 marks.

Kanji

/50

1

Part A

1x17= /17

Write the reading of the highlighted words in hiragana.

a 春子さんの家族(ぞく)は**四人**です。東京(きょう)に住んでいます。春子さんは高校**二年生**で、毎日おねえさんといっしょに**電車**で**学校**に行きます。一時間半ぐらいかかります。

b まだ日本語が**上手**じゃないですから、べんきょうが大変(たいへん)です。とくに、日本語でさくぶんを**書く**ことがとてもむずかしいです。だから、**英語**でさくぶんの書き方(かた)のせつめいがいります。それから、日本語の**会話**もれんしゅうしたいです。

c 毎年、四百五十万人ぐらいの**外国人**が日本に旅(りょ)行に行きます。日本で買い物をしたり、日本りょうりを食べたり、**見物**したりします。本州(しゅう)の**北**から、**南**まで、新幹線(かんせん)にのって、たくさんの**町**に行くことができます。

d **木曜日**に子どもがはしの上からあきかんを**川**になげたのを見ました。私は「あのあきかんはどこに行くのだろう。」と**思いました**。あのあきかんは川から、**海**に行って、ごみになると思いました。東京湾(きょうわん)の水がおせんされました。

Part B

2x4= /8

Match the information below with the corresponding passage from **Part A** by writing the appropriate letter.

(i) ☐ I wondered where the cans will go.

(ii) ☐ I want to practise my Japanese conversation too.

(iii) ☐ It takes about an hour and a half for Haruko to get to school everyday.

(iv) ☐ You can visit lots of cities by bullet train.

2

1x25= /25

Complete these sentences using the appropriate kanji.

a _____ 朝(あさ)、あさごはんを _____ べて、ジュースを _____ んで、__________ を _____ みます。
まい　た　の　しんぶん　よ

b お__________ は _____ ですか。__________________________ です。
なまえ　なん　やまぐち　あきこ

c __________ の_____ 転(てん)_____ にのったり、_____ の __________ にのったりします。
じぶん　じ　しゃ　ちち　くるま

d _____ 広(ひろ)くんのお _______ さんは ____________ 員(いん)で、_____ 阪(さか)に _____ んでいます。
たか　かあ　かいしゃ　おお　す

Listening

/50

1

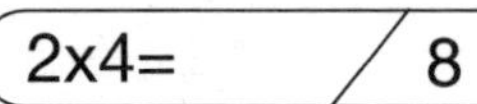

2x4= /8

Some students are chatting. Read through the responses first, then listen to each dialogue and circle the most appropriate one for each question.

a
- Toshio likes karate and was a member of the karate club last year.
- Toshio joined the karate club last year, but didn't like the competitions.
- Toshio likes doing karate, but doesn't think the club is very good.

b
- Mark can't read Japanese but likes looking at the pictures in comics.
- Mark can't understand everything he reads in Japanese comics.
- Mark can understand comics and thinks the pictures are interesting.

c
- Sheena prefers water skiing because she can swim well.
- Sheena can swim very well, but prefers skiing to waterskiing.
- Sheena prefers skiing because she can't swim well.

d
- Emi wants to do a university course in television animation.
- Emi has to study at university because she wants to become a journalist.
- Emi writes newspaper articles and does television reports, but wants to study at university in the future.

2

/16

Complete the note pad from the information you hear in the interviews in English or Japanese.

a /6

名前：__________

好きなスポーツ：__________

将来(しょうらい)、何になりたい？__________

りゆう *(reason)*：__________

____

b /10

名前：__________

何年生：__________

いちばん好きなかもく：__________

いちばん好きな先生：__________

どんな先生？__________

いちばんきらいな校則(こうそく)：__________

りゆう *(reason)*：__________

____

3

/26

Before you listen to Karen's speech about her trip to Japan, read through the questions and the vocabulary list. From the information you hear, answer the questions in English.

単語表(たんごひょう)

とちぎけん　Tochigi Prefecture

「日光(にっこう)を見ずして、けっこうと言うなかれ」
'You can't say you're content until you've seen Nikko'

たき	waterfall
高さ	height
17せいき	17th century
ところ	place

a Where is Tochigi Prefecture located? (2 marks)

____

b What kind of town is Nikko? (6 marks)

____

____

c What can you do there? (10 marks)

____

d How does Karen describe the Kegon waterfall? (4 marks)

____

____

e Who was Ieyasu Tokugawa? (4 marks)

____

Speaking

/50

1 

/25

With a partner, prepare **one** of the roles in the following dialogue. Present your dialogue to the class. Ask your teacher for the assessment criteria.

Don't forget about the use of *aizuchi.*

A: Greeting.
B: Greeting.
A: Find out what s/he thought of the movie last night on TV.
B: Say what you thought of the movie you watched on TV last night.
A: Ask what s/he thought of the main character.
B: Say what you thought of the main character.
A: Ask if s/he wants to go to see a particular movie with you on the weekend.
B: Say that your brother/sister saw it and say what sort of movie they thought it was.
A: Say what you've heard about the movie.
B: Agree to go on the weekend. Suggest when to meet.
A: Suggest where to meet and explain how to get there.
B: Ask where s/he is going now.
A: Say you are going to play a sport: say when and where you usually play.
B: Tell them that you want to join a sports team, but explain that because you have a part-time job, you don't have much free time.
A: Find out what her/his part-time job is, where and when s/he works.
B: Tell them about your part-time job including where and when you work. Also explain what you have to wear. Excuse yourself *(because you have to go to work now)*.
A: Farewell and say that you'll see her/him on the weekend.
B: Say goodbye.

2

/25

You are planning a day trip around your town or local area with your friend who is visiting from Japan. Use your knowledge of the area and research any further information you need.

Your task is to negotiate the activities and finalise the plans for the day with your friend, taking into account their interests and preferences. Your teacher may play the role of your friend for assessment purposes. Ask your teacher for the assessment criteria.

You should include the following:

- Suggest you spend a day together and decide on which day.
- Organise a time and place to meet.
- Suggest some appropriate activities, discuss them and decide on two.
- Work out the order that you are going to do the activities and the lunch arrangements.
- Suggest how you can get to your chosen activities.
- Give an estimate of the cost of the day's activities.
- Confirm the plans with your friend.

It will be up to you to show initiative in the conversation.

Reading

単語表

もんく complaint
たび journey
あちこち here and there

/50

25

1

Write a brief summary in English of the storyline of this manga. Ask your teacher for the assessment criteria.

2

/ 25

Read the web page about some tourist destinations in Victoria. Fill in the table in English or Japanese listing the features that appeal to you and the features that don't.

単語表

見つかる	to be found
金鉱 きんこう	gold mine
たいけんする	to experience
身長 しんちょう	height
海岸 かいがん	shore
す	burrow

ビクトリアしゅう

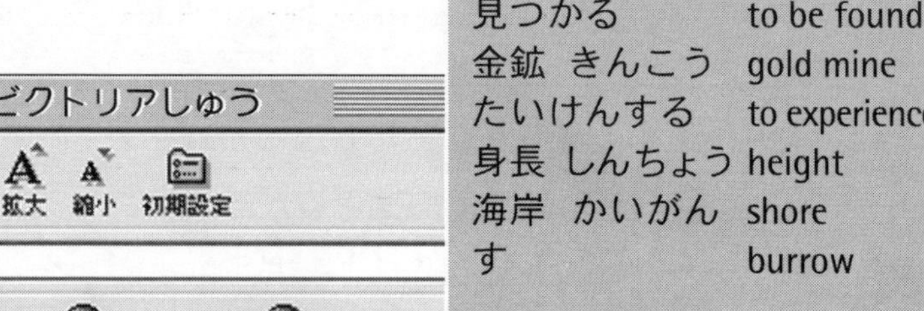

アドレス：

アップルコンピュータ　Mac OS　Power Macintosh　PowerBook　iMac

チャンネル　お気に入り　履歴　検索

ソブリン・ヒル

むかしビクトリアしゅうで金がたくさん見つかりました。そして、そのとき、新しくて、大きい町がたくさんできました。バララットはそのときできた「金鉱の町」です。

今バララットのソブリン・ヒルで１８５０年ごろの生活がたいけんできます。レストランで食べたり、金鉱の中に入ったり、ふるいゲームをしたりすることができます。大人も子どももたのしめます。

ソブリン・ヒルはメルボルンから１００キロぐらいのところにあって、車で一時間半かかります。電車でも、バララットに行けます。ツアーもあります。

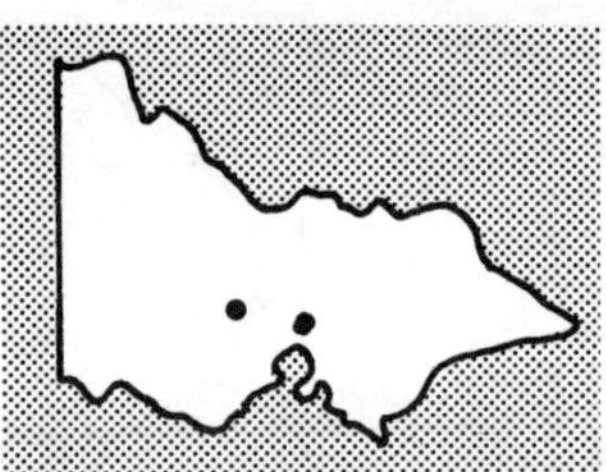

ペンギン・パレード

フィリップとうに行くと、フェアリーペンギンを見ることができます。フェアリーペンギンのしんちょうは３０センチぐらいで、小さくて、かわいいです。ひるの間、ペンギンは海でおよいだり、さかなを食べたりします。春から秋までは毎晩、海岸をあるいて、すにかえります。ちかくには動物園がありますから、パレードの前にそこでほかのオーストラリアの動物を見ることもできます。

フィリップとうは、ビクトリアしゅうの南のほうにあって、メルボルンから車で２時間ぐらいかかります。週末にはバスツアーもあります。

インターネットゾーン

a

	ちょうしょ (advantages)	たんしょ (disadvantages)
ソブリン・ヒル		
ペンギン・パレード		

b Decide which destination you would prefer to go to and give your reason in Japanese.

ソブリン・ヒルとペンギン・パレードとでは、どちらのほうがいいですか。
(りゆうをせつめいしてください。)

Writing /50

For this section, complete two tasks to total 50 marks.

1 /25

Write a reminder note including all the points listed for each of the following situations in Japanese.

a **大切(せつ)なきそく**

- I must not wear make-up.
- I must not chew gum.
- I must take off my shoes.
- I must not be late.
- I must leave home at 8:00am and arrive at school at 8:30am.

b **テニス**

- Play tennis at 5:30 on Wednesday.
- Meet Hisako in front of the library at 5:00.
- The library is north of Wyndham (ウィンダム) station.
- Walk straight ahead and turn left at the third corner.
- If I go straight along the street, I'll see the library on the left.

c **クリスマスプレゼント**

- Sam said that she likes long boots.
- Dad wants a book about sumo wrestling.
- I will probably buy Peter's birthday present tomorrow.
- Jake needs a new computer so that he can use the internet.
- Mum said she wants a big television, but it's too expensive.

2

/25

Produce the text for an informative pamphlet on the environment by writing briefly on some or all of the following topics. You may use the title, section headings and questions as a guide to develop your writing. The pamphlet should be about 200-250じ. Ask your teacher for the assessment criteria and the *genkooyooshi*.

ちきゅうにやさしく

Topics	Suggestions
ごみ	きれいな町ときたない町とでは、どちらのほうがいいですか。 川はきれいですか。海はきれいですか。
リサイクル	何がリサイクルできますか。どうして？いつ？だれが？ リサイクルの物から何がつくれますか。
わりばし	わりばしとはしとでは、どちらのほうがいいですか。 なぜ？

Notes: ______________________________

____

____

____

____

3

/25

Choose either Part A or B.

Part A

Write an informative newsletter article for a student publication on **one** of the following topics. The length of the piece should be about 400じ (one page of げんこうようし). Ask your teacher for the assessment criteria and the *genkooyooshi.*

- 日本の学校
- 私のアルバイト
- *(destination)* への旅(りょ)行
- 大好きなスポーツせんしゅ

Part B

Write a personal diary entry of about 400じ (one page of げんこうようし) relating to **one** of the following topics.

- 夏休みに ・*(destination)* への旅(りょ)行
- 日本の高校でのはじめての日

Notes: ______________________________

____

____

____

漢字の書き方

(かんじ の か き かた)

This is the kanji section of the Workbook. For each unit in your Student Book there are exercises in this section. There are four parts per unit; stroke order, reading/pronunciation practice, writing practice and a fun game/puzzle. To begin, here is a puzzle which reviews the kanji from Obentoo 1 and 2.

1

Find the kanji readings in the puzzle and discover the question from the remaining characters. Answer the question using as many kanji as you can.

てんきえんなでこやまのぼりおね
いきましたんぐどあみやでかとん
はるやすみじちもめますんいこが
かゆでんきスタンドすいしまのじ
いきでんわしてくださいゃすこょ
もおふなんまんどようびみゆきう
のんゆちいりぐちくるまぎきんな
すなのいがごまんたかかったよか
きうひさしょうがっこうにかうや
なえすいおんなのこいてほっびま
きにじゅっぷんまえちんんてでが
さんじはんひだりながきおいなく
あきすいようびごまつよおまかえ
おおきくないすねえかほあすにん
はちじゅうえんんなつうめしたに

好きな
金曜日
高かった
買い物(もの)
山登(のぼ)り
名(な)前
天気予報(よほう)
年賀状(がじょう)
小学校(がっこう)
秋
左
入口
下に
中に
中山学園(がくえん)
五年
右
天気
一月
三時半
水曜日
春休み
何時
上に
電話(わ)してください
行きました
冬の日
男の子
雨
雪女
子ども
五万
夏
円
八十円
電車
見ます
何万
出口
女の子
大雨
車
小さい
安い
買います
土曜日
十分前
日本
電気スタンド
大きくない
買っています

Answers can only be found across or down.

単語表 (たんごひょう)

年賀状　ねんがじょう
New Year card

Message question: ______________________

____

Your answer: ______________________

____

Unit 1

1

かんじをれんしゅうしてください。

新	新							新	新
聞	聞							聞	聞
私	私							私	私
読	読							読	読

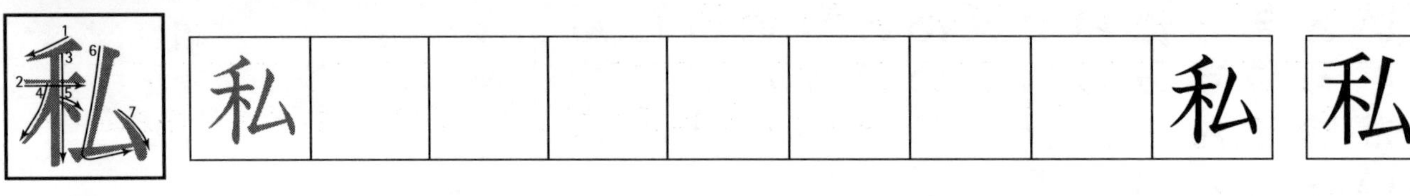

2

Read aloud the following passage written by Kota to complete the questions in English.

月曜日から、金曜日まで、私は学校(がっこう)のあとで、しゅくだいをして、ラジオを聞きます。そして、ごはんのあとで、テレビを見ます。毎週(まいしゅう)、日曜日に、新聞で一週間(しゅうかん)のテレビばんぐみひょうを見ます。Xファイルやフレンズやクイズばんぐみが大好きです。でも、今週(こんしゅう)から Xファイルもいちばん好きなクイズばんぐみも水曜日の八時半にはじまります。どうしましょう？

Be careful to pronounce each character correctly in context.
The hiragana added to kanji to make whole words is called *okurigana*. For example, 聞**きます**.

単語表(たんひょう)

テレビばんぐみひょう — television programme guide
はじまります — starts

a What does Koota do after school every day?

(i) ______________________________

(ii) ______________________________

b What does Koota do on Sundays?

____

c What is the problem from this week onwards?

____

3

Write out the following passge on げんこうようし using the kanji you know from *Obentoo 1* and 2 and the new ones from this unit (the words in bold should be written in kanji). Remember the rules for using げんこうようし (refer *Obentoo 2 Student Book*, pages 68–9).

　わたしは、まい**にち**、**しんぶん**を**よみます**。きょう、おもしろいきじが**ふたつ**ありました。

　まず、**あたらしいくるま**についてのきじでした。その**くるま**はトヨタの**くるま**で、はやくて、安全（あんぜん）です。エアバッグや、ナビゲーションシステムや、パワーステアリングなどがあります。**しんぶん**のしゃしんはあおいクーペでした。**わたし**はクーペが**すき**です。でも、その**くるま**はすこし**たかかった**です。

　つぎのきじはウォルト·ディズニーについてでした。ウォルト·ディズニーはアメリカ**じん**で、アニメをつくりました。**わたし**は**こども**の**とき**に、ディズニーのアニメをたくさん**みました**。**なつやすみ**にかぞくと、とうきょうディズニーランドに**いきたい**です。

　きょうの**しんぶん**はとてもおもしろかったです。

単語表（たんごひょう）

きじ	*(newspaper)* article
まず	first
〜について	about
あんぜんな	safe
つぎ	next
こどものとき	when I was a child

(とき *is a new reading for the kanji* じ *meaning o'clock/time*)

Don't forget the *okurigana* to complete the words!

Unit 2

1

かんじをれんしゅうしてください。

今	今							今	今
週	週							週	週
毎	毎							毎	毎
間	間							間	間
手	手							手	手
住	住							住	住
名	名							名	名
々	々							々	々

2

Match the following words with their reading and meaning as in the example.

住んでいます •	• ゆうめいな •	• *(for)* two hours
時々 •	• じょうずな •	• *(for)* two years
下手な •	• ときどき •	• today
山下さん •	• まいにち •	• Mr/Ms Yamashita
今日 •	• へたな •	• sometimes
今週 •	• てがみ •	• live
今年 •	• すんでいます •	• good at
上手な •	• きょう •	• *(for)* two weeks
手紙(がみ) •	• ひとびと •	• famous
毎日 •	• ねんねん •	• this week
人々 •	• こんしゅう •	• year by year
二週間 •	• にしゅうかん •	• this year
上に •	• まいしゅう •	• every day
毎週 •	• なまえ •	• people
二年間 •	• にじかん •	• not skilled at
年々 •	• いま •	• letter
二時間 •	• うえに •	• now
名前 •	• にねんかん •	• every week
今 •	• やましたさん •	• on top of
有(ゆう)名な •	• ことし •	• name

3

Write the following interview in Japanese in your exercise book or on げんこうようし, using as many kanji as you can.

Yukiko: Hello. What is your name?
Akiko: My name is Akiko Yamanaka.
Yukiko: May I interview you?
Akiko: Yes, that's fine.
Yukiko: What sports do you like?
Akiko: I like water skiing.
Yukiko: Do you live near the beach?
Akiko: Yes, I live in Ito.
Yukiko: How long have you been water skiing?
Akiko: About five years. My father likes water skiing too and he is good at it.
Yukiko: When do you do it?
Akiko: Every week. Sometimes we go on Saturday, but this week we're going on Sunday.
Yukiko: Thank you (*for today's interview*).

4

If you have access to a computer which has a Japanese word processing program, you can word process in Japanese using a standard computer keyboard. If you use a Japanese ワープロ(*word processor*), you can type directly using the kana symbols. A ワープロ is the equivalent of a typewriter and the keyboard is the same for electronic dictionaries etc.

ワープロのキーボード

These are the positions of the basic keys on a ワープロ keyboard.

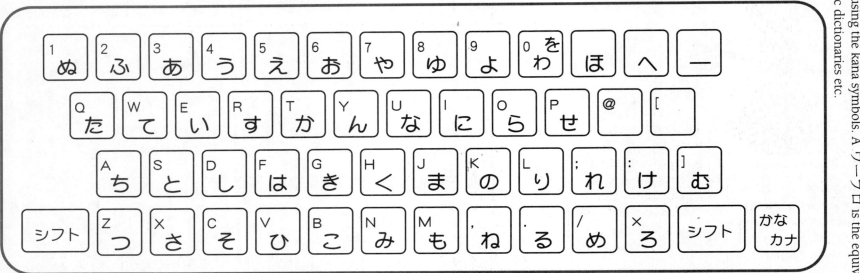

1 ぬ	2 ふ	3 あ	4 う	5 え	6 お	7 や	8 ゆ	9 よ	0 を わ	ほ	へ	ー	
Q た	W て	E い	R す	T か	Y ん	U な	I に	O ら	P せ	@	[		
A ち	S と	D し	F は	G き	H く	J ま	K の	L り	; れ	: け	] む		
シフト	Z っ	X さ	C そ	V ひ	B こ	N み	M も	, ね	. る	/ め	× ろ	シフト	かな カナ

You will notice that characters using てんてん(が、じ、ぶ) or まる(ぽ) don't appear on this keyboard.

For characters using てんてん, key in the base character plus @. For example, か followed by @ becomes が.

For characters using まる, key in the base character plus [. For example, は followed by [becomes ぱ. Small ゃ、ゅ、ょ and っ are made by using the shift key, then the character.

The extra characters or letters attached to each key are accessed by changing the mode. On this keyboard, Japanese can be written by typing in hiragana using the kana mode or by sounding out each character and typing it using the ローマ字(じ) mode.

There are some differences between the positions of some symbols on this keyboard and the standard English keyboard. Can you find them?
Why do you think the kana characters are arranged this way?

The message below has been typed in using the kana mode, but is presented showing the equivalent English key. For example, 3GB=あきこ. Using the keyboard, decipher the message from the English keys into kana. Then write it out using as many kanji as you can.

0 Q D K S M Q@ A K U J 5 F 3 G B X Y W@
R　3 G B X Y F X Y , Y　T Y H@ O E U B@7 I
R Y W@ E J R　J E D shift 8 4 3 G B X Y I
W@ Y 0 shift 0 D J R S G S@ G W T@ N
shift 0 T G J R　G shift 9 4 F 3 G B X Y K Q
Y D@ shift 9 4 V@ W@ R　P Y D shift84 3G
B X Y I 8 4 V@Y G shift9 H W@**2**　[**; P@Y S**
shift 0 T E J D Q

Study the differences between 0 (zero) and O *(capital 'o')* and 1 *(one)* and I *(capital 'i')*.

The bold section is in katakana. To do this on the keyboard, press the かな／カナ key (*bottom right key*) then press it again to return to hiragana.

Particle を can be typed using shift+0 (*zero*)

The space indicates the end of a sentence.

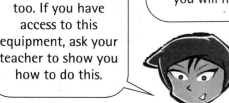

Of course ワープロ and Japanese word processing programs can produce kanji too. If you have access to this equipment, ask your teacher to show you how to do this.

ヒント！ When you have finished using all the kanji that you know, the message should take １０９げんこうようし squares (5 lines plus 9 squares). This includes 6 full stops and 2 commas which you will need to add as you go.

Unit 3

1

かんじをれんしゅうしてください。

先	先								先	先
生	生								生	生
学	学								学	学
校	校								校	校
家	家								家	家
自	自								自	自
出	出								出	出
入	入								入	入

2

Erica is an exchange student living in Japan. She is writing to a Japanese friend living in New Zealand. Read Erica's letter and then answer the questions in Japanese.

さなえさんへ、

こんにちは。お元気ですか。私も元気です。

ニュージーランドは秋ですね。今、日本は春で、さくらがたくさんさいています。とてもきれいで、すばらしいです。毎日、たくさんの人がこうえんや川のそばに行って、花見をします。私は先週末に学校の友だちとこうえんに行って、ピクニックをしました。

日本の三月と四月はいそがしいですね。三月に、学校のそつぎょうしきがあって、四月に入学式があります。ホストファミリーのおにいさんは高校をそつぎょうして、今月大学に入学します。いもうとさんのさつきちゃんも、小学校のそつぎょうしきに出ました。四月から中学一年生になります。私は高校二年生になりますから、入学式はありません。

ホストファミリーのお父さんは会社員で、お母さんは英会話の先生です。じゅくで、中学生におしえています。私は時々じゅくにあそびに行きます。日本では、小学生もじゅくで英語やさんすうをべんきょうするんですね。びっくりしました。中学生や高校生もじゅくに行っていますね。ほとんどの学生はじゅけんをしなければなりませんから、じゅくに行くんですね。大変ですね。

私はけんどうぶに入っています。ほとんど毎日、学校のあとで、れんしゅうします。私はスポーツが好きで、日本のでんとうてきなスポーツをしたかったですから、けんどうはぶに入りました。友だちもたくさんできて、れんしゅうはたのしいですが、先生はとてもきびしくて、こわいです。もちろん、れんしゅうにおくれて行ってはだめです。

学校では、かもくがたくさんありますね。いちばん好きなかもくは社会です。でも、むずかしくて、大変です。国語もむずかしいですね。ぜんぜん分かりませんから、いつも自分で、かんじのれんしゅうをします。さなえさんも、がんばっていますか。留学は大変ですが、いろいろなべんきょうができますから、いいですね。留学してよかったです。

ニュージーランドの高校生活はどうですか。

では、お元気で。おからだに気をつけてください。

みなさんによろしくおつたえください。

２００２年4月1日

エリカより

a 今、日本では、どのきせつですか。それから、ニュージーランドはどのきせつですか。

b たくさんの人はこうえんや川のそばで何をしますか。

c エリカさんは週末に何をしましたか。

d なぜ三月と四月はいそがしいですか。

e ホストファミリーのおにいさんはどこに入学しますか。

f ホストファミリーのお父さんとお母さんのおしごとは何ですか。

g 小学生はじゅくで、どんなかもくをべんきょうしますか。

h エリカさんはどんなクラブに入っていますか。どうですか。

i エリカさんは学校で、どんなかもくをべんきょうしていますか。いちばん好きなかもくは何ですか。

j エリカさんの留学生活はどうですか。

単語表

さく	to bloom	英会話 えいかいわ	English conversation
花見をする はなみをする	flower viewing	じゅく	cram school
そつぎょうしき	graduation ceremony	さんすう	arithmetic
入学式 にゅうがくしき	entrance ceremony	ほとんどの	almost
そつぎょうする	to graduate	じゅけんをする	to take a test
入学する にゅうがくする	to enter	生活 せいかつ	lifestyle
しき	ceremony	もちろん	of course
会社員 かいしゃいん	company employee	社会 しゃかい	society
		おくれる	to be late
		国語 こくご	Japanese language

3 Magic kanji corners

You may have wondered about the empty boxes at the top of each page in your Workbook. To make your own Magic kanji corners, choose the kanji that you have the most trouble remembering and write the kanji in the boxes stroke by stroke (refer to pages 2–5). Before you begin, check that your stroke order is correct by referring to the appropriate unit kanji section in your Student Book.

4

Part A

Write these sentences in Japanese on a sheet of げんこうようし. Start a new line for each sentence. It is important that you use as much kanji as you can. When you have finished, check your sentences are correct.

Last week I read a comic book.

I listened to the news before dinner.

I bought five cans of cola at the shop.

Lots of newspapers are published in America.

That man is a sumo wrestler and he's fat. (ふとっています is fat)

I like resting on the weekends.

Every night after a small snack, I watch TV. (毎晩(ばん) every night)

The boys mucked around after the movie.

I love maths.

She's Ms Takayama and she's a physical education teacher.

My family goes to the beach each year. (毎年 every year)

I ate breakfast at 8:05.

I join a sports club every year.

Her name is Haruko Murata.

I came to school by bike today.

May I phone my friend?

Natalie is Canadian and she's good at skiing.

It was a Japanese test.

I used the new, expensive computer.

There was a lamp (*electric*) on top of the table.

Part B Kanji Super Challenge

If you have successfully completed **Part A**, there is a Super Challenge Puzzle that can extend your kanji recognition. Ask your teacher for details.

Unit 5

1

かんじをれんしゅうしてください。

母	母								母	母
父	父								父	父
英	英								英	英
語	語								語	語
話	話								話	話
書	書								書	書
来	来								来	来
会	会								会	会

2

Part A

Read the following job advertisements from a Japanese community newspaper in Australia and note down in your exercise book the main requirements for each job in point form. Discuss these points with a partner and how you might demonstrate the skills needed for each job.

1

てんいんぼしゅう

人に会うことが好きですか。あなたはあかるくて、まじめな人で、英語が上手な人ですか。有名で、すてきなめんぜいてんではたらきませんか。毎週土日、一時から五時までです。きょうみがありますか。電話してください。

電話番号：（０２）９０８１　７７５５

単語表

てんいんぼしゅう	shop assistant wanted
まじめな	hard working
めんぜいてん	duty free shop
きょうみ	interest

2

ベビーシッター

子どもが好きですか。ほうかごはひまですか。子どもたちは六才と八才で、英語がすこしできます。

電話番号：（０３）９２３２　５６４５

単語表

ほうかご	after school

3

ツアーガイド

旅行が好きですか。ツアーガイドをしてみたいですか。日本語と英語が話せますか。

日本人かんこうきゃくをくうこうで出迎えて、町をあんないします。会社で、トレーニングができます。時給はとてもいいです。

Ｅメールをください。

電話番号：（０３）９６６９　１４７２

Ｅメール：travelmate@smallpond.com.au

単語表

くうこう	airport
出迎える でむかえる	to meet
あんないする	to show around

4

家庭教師

中学生の息子に英語のさくぶんの書き方と英会話をおしえてください。息子はあかるいせいかくで、学校が大好きです。でも、英語が上手じゃないですから、べんきょうが大変です。毎週月曜日と木曜日に一時間半ぐらいのレッスンをしてください。

来週、会いに来られますか。

電話番号：（０３）９９８７　６８６５

単語表

せいかく	personality

Part B

Read the self-introductions to work out which of the positions in **Part A** is best for each person. Write the number in the box.

単語表（たんひょう）

とうろん	debating
大会 たいかい	competition
修学旅行 しゅうがくりょこう	school trip

私は高校二年生で、日本語が大好きです。学校のとうろんクラブに入っています。先週、大会（たいかい）に出て、チャンピオンになりました。来年、日本に修（しゅう）学旅（りょ）行に行きますから、アルバイトをさがしています。

こんにちは。私はベリンダです。家族（ぞく）は六人で、九才（さい）のおとうとと五才（さい）のいもうとがいます。週末（まつ）はスポーツでいそがしいですが、学校のあとはひまです。新しいふくがほしいですから、アルバイトをさがしています。

ぼくは小学校一年生の時から、日本語をべんきょうしています。去（きょ）年、日本に一年間留（りゅう）学しましたから、日本語ができます。日本人に会うことが好きです。週末（まつ）のアルバイトをさがしています。

ぼくは高校一年生です。話すことが好きですから、人に会うことはたのしいです。母はオーストラリア人で、父は日本人ですから、英語も日本語も話せます。平日（へいじつ）の昼間（ひるま）はひまで、アルバイトがしたいです。

単語表（たんひょう）

平日の昼間 へいじつのひるま	weekday afternoon

単語表（たんひょう）

さがす	to look for

3

Write out the following sentences using kanji. The bold words are to be written in kanji.

a **えいご**が**はな**せますか。

b **はは**は**せんせい**で、**えいかいわ**をおしえています。

c **とも**だちに**あ**うことが**す**きです。

d **ちち**はジャーナリストで、**まいにちしんぶん**のきじを**か**きます。

4

Complete the chart in Japanese by filling in the appropriate time word in the sequence. Use kanji wherever possible.

	Past	Present	Future
a	きのう		明日
b	先週		
c		今月	
d	去（きょ）年		

5

You have already learned that kanji are made up of a set number of strokes. Complete the table to write **eleven** words in kanji. The first one has been done for you.

Total number of strokes	English	Kanji word
9	Father's day	父の日
11	next month	
11	teacher	
13	next year	
19	conversation	
19	mother tongue	
21	primary school	
22	English	
23	Japanese	
23	dictionary	辞(じ)
26	telephone	
27	newspaper	

Father's Day is written using a combination of kanji and hiragana, so count the hiragana strokes too.

6 Kanji card games

If you have four sets of kanji cards for the kanji that you know, you can adapt many standard card games. Some easy examples are: Concentration, Go Fish, Snap, Competition Snap etc. Ask your teacher for details of these games or you could try inventing your own card game! All of these games will help you remember the kanji you have learnt. As you learn new kanji in each unit, add them into your deck of kanji cards.

Unit 6

1

かんじをれんしゅうしてください。

北	北							北	北
南	南							南	南
東	東							東	東
西	西							西	西
町	町							町	町
物	物							物	物
食	食							食	食
飲	飲							飲	飲

2

Match the kanji words with their hiragana reading and English meaning.

買い物 •	• ひがし •	• to eat
外食 •	• とうきょう •	• to drink
南西 •	• のむ •	• east
東 •	• がいしょく •	• shopping
東京 •	• かいもの •	• eating out
南アメリカ •	• みなみアメリカ •	• food and drink
南アフリカ •	• たべる •	• sightseeing
飲食物 •	• なんせい •	• southwest
見物 •	• けんぶつ •	• Tokyo
食べる •	• いんしょくぶつ •	• South Africa
飲む •	• みなみアフリカ •	• South America

3

What do these signs mean? Read them aloud with a partner.

東口

買い物センター

おいしい！
食べほうだい！

西口

お手洗い（あら）

西川ビル

地下鉄（ちてつ）

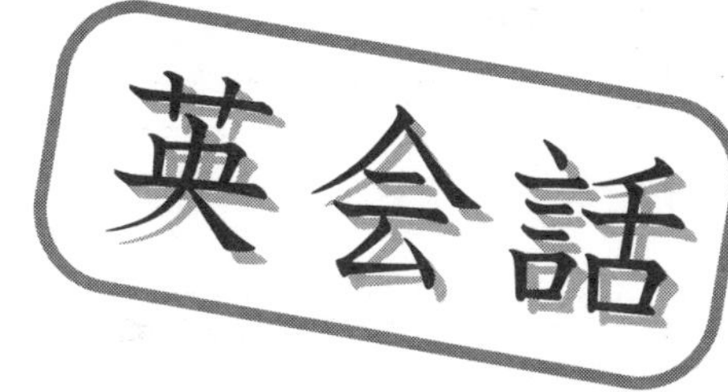

4

Read the extract from a travel brochure below and answer the questions in Japanese as fully as you can.

北海道に来ませんか

北海道は本州の北にあります。本州から飛行機や電車やフェリーで行けます。もちろん、飛行機はべんりですが、電車のほうがおもしろいです。新幹線で盛岡まで行って、盛岡からとっきゅうで札幌まで行きます。本州と北海道の間には、青函トンネルがあって、海の下をはしります。青森から、フェリーで行くこともできます。北海道は人口がすくないですが、自然がおおいです。

札幌は北海道でいちばん大きい町です。冬に雪まつりがあります。雪まつりでは、雪で大きいモニュメントをたくさんつくります。せかい中の建物や有名人のかおなどです。

それから、おいしいレストランがたくさんあります。北海道は食べ物がおいしいです。ラーメンやジンギスカンが有名ですが、いちばん有名な食べ物はいしかりなべです。さけ・こんぶ・やさい・とうふをつかって、みそでりょうりします。

函館も有名です。北海道の南西にあって、海のそばにあります。天気がいいと、函館山から町がよく見えます。よるのけしきはとてもきれいです。

札幌の東に富良野という町があって、有名で、すばらしいスキーじょうがあります。スキーのあとで、あついおんせんに入って、くつろぐことができます。

北海道は自然がとてもきれいです。あそびに来てください。

a 北海道はどこにありますか。

____

b どうやって、北海道まで行きますか。

____

c 青函トンネルはどこにありますか。

____

____

d 札幌はどんな町ですか。

____

____

e 冬に何がありますか。

____

f いちばん有名なりょうりは何ですか。

____

単語表

Place names

北海道	ほっかいどう
本州	ほんしゅう
盛岡	もりおか
札幌	さっぽろ
函館	はこだて
青函トンネル	せいかんトネル
富良野	ふらの

もちろん	of course
とっきゅう	limited express train
はしる	to run
自然 しぜん	nature
ジンギスカン	Mongolian BBQ
さけ	salmon
こんぶ	kelp
やさい	vegetables
とうふ	bean curd
みそ	bean paste
そば	near by/close by
スキーじょう	ski slopes
～という町	a town called...
くつろぐ	to relax

g 函館(はこだて)はどこにありますか。

____

h 北海道(ほっかいどう)のどこに有(ゆう)名で、すばらしいスキーじょうがありますか。スキーのあとで何をすることができますか。______________________________

____

5

Write the following sentences in Japanese using kanji. Don't forget to add the *okurigana* if necessary. Then write the English meaning in the space provided.

とうなん is written in kanji as 東南. It is a special reading for 東南アジア.

a **にほん**の**たべもの**では**なに**が**すき**ですか。

____

____

b どんな**のみもの**がいちばん**すき**ですか。

____

____

c **ひがしぐち**を**でて**、**みぎ**にまがると、デパートが**みえます**。

____

____

d **にし**オーストラリアは**おおきくて**、ひろいところです。

____

____

e しょう**らい**、**にほん**に**いって**、**にほんご**をつかってみたいです。

____

____

f **きた**アメリカに**いきました**が、**ことしみなみ**アメリカに**いって**みたいです。

____

____

g **とう**きょう**はおおきいまち**ですから、がい**しょく**することはたのしいです。

____

____

h **とうなん**アジアに**いって**、**けんぶつ**したいです。

____

____

6

Taku, Ayumi and Kylie are all going to town. They each start from different places and go to where they want to by following the directions at each block. Trace their routes on the map and find out what each one wants to do in town by identifying their destinations. Answer the question below about each one in English.

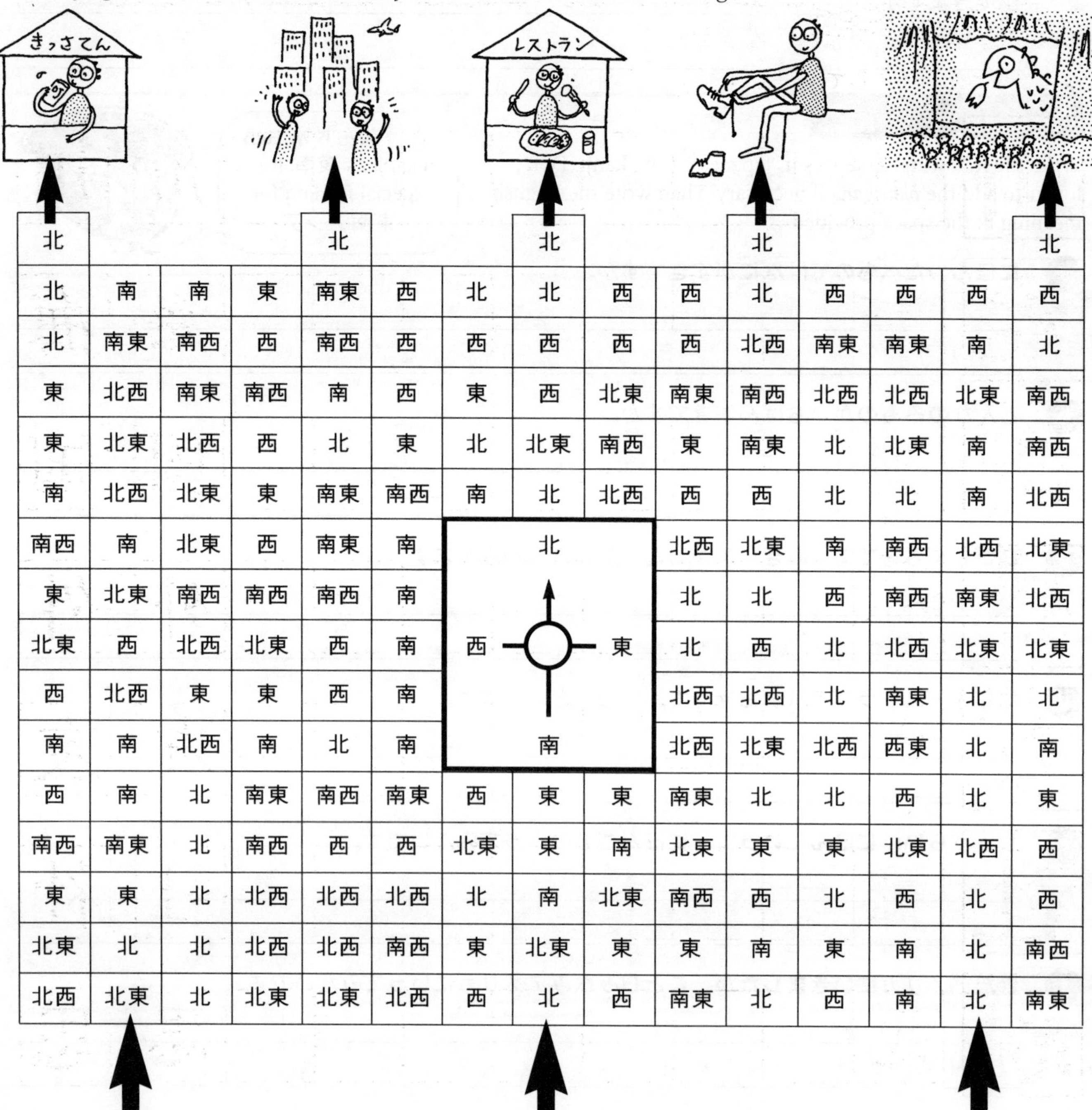

北				北			北			北				北
北	南	南	東	南東	西	北	北	西	西	北	西	西	西	西
北	南東	南西	西	南西	西	西	西	西	西	北西	南東	南東	南	北
東	北西	南東	南西	南	西	東	西	北東	南東	南西	北西	北西	北東	南西
東	北東	北西	西	北	東	北	北東	南西	東	南東	北	北東	南	南西
南	北西	北東	東	南東	南西	南	北	北西	西	西	北	北	南	北西
南西	南	北東	西	南東	南		北		北西	北東	南	南西	北西	北東
東	北東	南西	南西	南西	南				北	北	西	南西	南東	北西
北東	西	北西	北東	西	南	西		東	北	西	北	北西	北東	北東
西	北西	東	東	西	南				北西	北西	北	南東	北	北
南	南	北西	南	北	南		南		北西	北東	北西	西東	北	南
西	南	北	南東	南西	南東	西	東	東	南東	北	北	西	北	東
南西	南東	北	南西	西	西	北東	東	南	北東	東	東	北東	北西	西
東	東	北	北西	北西	北西	北	南	北東	南西	西	北	西	北	西
北東	北	北	北西	北西	南西	東	北東	東	東	南	東	南	北	南西
北西	北東	北	北東	北東	北西	西	北	西	南東	北	西	南	北	南東

What do Taku, Ayumi and Kylie want to do in town?

a たく: ______________________________

b あゆみ: ______________________________

c カイリー: ______________________________

4

Write the following sentences in Japanese using kanji that you know. Also give the English meaning in the space provided.

a オーストラリアはおおきくて、ひろいくにですね。

b にほんのかいしゃいんはながいじかんはたらくとおもいます。

c ゆうこさんはうみがいちばんすきだといいました。

d わたしはにほんにいって、たのしいおもいでがたくさんできました。

e ちちはちゅうごくじんで、はははにほんじんです。

f やまかわせんせいはごねんかん、かいがいにすんだといいました。

g わたしはいいともだちがいることはたいせつだとおもいます。

h ホストのおとうさんはにほんかいがきれいなうみだといいました。

5

You are staying with Mari and her family for a year. While you are there, Mari's family is planning to take a holiday in February, but they are having difficulty deciding whether they will go to Australia or Italy. Mari is collating everyone's preferences to find out the most popular choice.

Part A

You are to help Mari by substituting the kanji from the grid for the reference locations in the sentences. Write out the sentences using the kanji from the grid on げんこうようし.

Part B

Decide which destination you think the family should go to. With a partner, discuss the reasons for your choice and then in your exercise book write a brief explanation in Japanese (include the reasons for your decision).

	一	二	三	四	五	六	七	八	九	十
あ	新	読	名	来	間	入	町	自	先	語
い	会	水	半	今	英	川	学	言	日	九
う	食	私	七	話	手	外	三	社	物	西
え	友	八	生	上	何	木	書	月	下	左
お	年	火	国	出	四	毎	父	千	六	女
か	時	万	々	東	分	右	土	海	天	雨
き	春	北	金	行	五	夏	電	前	中	高
く	秋	子	車	母	冬	円	休	大	思	本
け	気	買	小	十	南	百	山	曜	人	雪
こ	家	聞	飲	男	見	二	週	校	好	住

（う２）はオーストラリア（け９）です。（き６）（く２）さんはオーストラリアで、（う２）の（こ１）族（ぞく）に（い１）えます。いいかんがえだと（く９）いませんか。

（き６）（く２）さんのおにいさんといもうとさんは（い７）（こ８）で（い５）（あ１０）をべんきょうしています。お（く４）さんも（い５）（あ１０）がすこし（う４）せます。

（き６）（く２）さんは、（く７）みに（か８）でおよいだり、（い６）でつりをしたりしたいと（い８）いました。

お（く４）さんは、（う６）（あ３）の（う８）（い１）はとてもおもしろいと（い８）いました。イタリアには、とてもふるい建（たて）（う９）があって、でんとうてきな教（きょう）（い１）や博物館（はくぶつかん）などがたくさんあります。

お（お７）さんは、（か９）（け１）がわるいのはきらいだと（い８）いました。

いもうとさんは、イタリアの（う１）べ（う９）が（く８）（こ９）きだと（い８）いました。

おにいさんは、オペラが（こ９）きで、イタリア（あ１０）がすこし（か５）かります。

オーストラリア旅（りょ）（き４）とイタリア旅（りょ）（き４）とではどちらのほうがいいですか。

Japanese-English word lists

Unit 1

アクションえいが	action movie
あそこ	over there
アニメ	cartoon
あまい	sweet
あんぜんな	safe
いろいろな	various
インタービューします	to interview
うりば	shop counter
おしえます	to teach
おそくなって ごめんなさい	sorry I'm late
かいてきな	comfortable
かしゅ	singer
かっこわるい	ugly/idiotic
ギター	guitar
ゲスト	guest
コメディー	comedy
こんなに	this much
さいきん	recently
しっています	I know
ジャイアンツ	Giants
しらないこと	things I don't know
すくない	few
セーラームーン	Sailor Moon
せんしゅ	player
ぜんぶ	all/the whole
たいてい	usually
たいへんな	terrible
つきます	to arrive
どうしましょうか	what shall we do?
ところ	place
ながい	long
なりたくうこう	Narita Airport *(Tokyo)*
なります	to become
にぎやかな	lively/crowded
はじまります	*(it)* starts
はじまるまで	until *(it)* starts
はじめは	at first
ハルマゲドン	Armageddon
ばんぐみ	*(television/radio)* programme
ファミコン	*(family)* computer games
ふるい	old
へんな	strange
ポケモン	Pokemon *(Pocket Monster)*
まんがか	comic writer
もんだい	problem
ラッセル·クロー	Russell Crowe
らんぼうな	violent/rough
れんしゅう (する)	practice *(to practise)*
ロマンチックな	romantic
わらって Hey!Hey!	"Laugh Ha!Ha!" *(television programme)*

新	あたら(しい)、しん	new
聞	ききます、ぶん	to hear, to listen
私	わたし、し	I, me
読	よ(みます)、どく	to read

会います	あいます	to meet
新しい	あたらしい	new
一度	いちど	once/one time
宇宙人	うちゅうじん	aliens
海	うみ	sea
英語	えいご	English
階	かい	counters for floor level
買い物	かいもの	shopping
会話	かいわ	conversation
書きます	かきます	to write
家族	かぞく	family
漢字	かんじ	kanji
来ます	きます	to come
国際的な	こくさいてきな	international
子ども	こども	child
週末	しゅうまつ	weekend
主人公	しゅじんこう	main character
将来	しょうらい	the future
上手な	じょうずな	good at/skillful
新聞	しんぶん	newspaper
生徒	せいと	student
せかい中で	せかいじゅうで	throughout the world
食べます	たべます	to eat
単語	たんご	words
月	つき	moon
出ます	でます	to come out/to be published
動物園	どうぶつえん	zoo
友だち	ともだち	friend
人気がある	にんきがある	to be popular
日記	にっき	diary
日本のこと	にほんのこと	things about Japan
話します	はなします	to talk/speak
毎週	まいしゅう	every week
毎日	まいにち	every day
毎晩	まいばん	every night
見てみましょう	みてみましょう	let's try looking

有名な	ゆうめいな	famous
読みます	よみます	to read
留学生	りゅうがくせい	exchange student
分かりやすい	わかりやすい	easy to understand
私	わたし	I/me

Unit 2

あいきどう	aikido *(martial art)*
あこがれる	to be attracted by
あね	older sister *(your own)*
～い	ranked
インターネット	internet
インタビュー	interview
ウエイト	a weight
ウエイトトレーニング	weight training
ウインドウ	window *(computer)*
うつ	to hit
エキスパート	expert
おいくつ	how old?
オートバイ	motor bike
オープン	open
おしえる	to teach
おやつ	snack
かえってから	after returning home
かえり	on the way home
かつ	to win
かつどう	activity
カメラ	camera
きじ	article
きびしい	strict
キャンセル	cancel
きゅうどう	Japanese archery
きる	to wear *(upper half)*
キロ	kilogram
こ	counter for round things
ゴーカート	go-kart
(六時) ごろ	around *(six o'clock)*
サーキット	circuit *(aerobics)*
サーチ	search *(internet)*
さんぽ	walking
しあい	match
Jリーグ	J league *(Japanese soccer league)*
ジム	gym
じゅうどう	judo
しゅるい	kind/sort
しょくぎょう	occupation
しんちょう	height/stature
ステップ	step *(aerobics)*
スピン	spin *(aerobics)*
すもう	sumo wrestling
すもうべや	sumo training dormitory
セーター	jumper/sweater
せんしゅ	player
たいじゅう	body weight
だから	therefore
チームスポーツ	team sport
チャットルーム	chatroom
ちゃんこなべ	vegetable and meat hotpot
チャンピオン	champion
(～に) ついて	about
つぎ	next
つよい	strong
とくべつな	special
トーナメント	tournament
とる	to take *(photos, notes)*
なかったから	because there was not
ねる	to sleep
はしる	to run
パット	patting
ハンディキャップ	handicap
パンプ	pump *(aerobics)*
ひく	to play *(musical instrument)*
ビジターチケット	visitor ticket
ピッチャー	pitcher
ビュー	view *(computer)*
ひるね	nap
ピンポン	ping pong
ファイル	file
～ぶ	club
ぶいん	club member
ぶじゅつ	martial arts
ふとっている	to be fat
ふとる	to get fat
プロ	professionals
ヘビーメタル	heavy metal
ホームページ	homepage *(internet)*
ほかに	apart from
ポップス	pops
マインスイーパー	Mine Sweeper *(computer game)*
まつ	to wait
まるい	round
まわり	around
メール	mail *(computer)*
ゆうしょうする	to win/to be victorious
ヨガ	yoga
りきし	sumo wrestler
リレハンメルオリンピック	Lillehammer Olympics

今	いま、こん、きん	now
週	しゅう	week
毎	ごと、まい	every
間	あいだ、かん	duration, between
手	て、しゅ、ず	hand
住	す(む)、じゅう	to live
名	な、めい、みょう	name
々		kanji repetition sign

明日	あした	tomorrow
家	いえ、うち	house/home
今	いま	now
居間	いま	lounge room
入れる	いれる	to put in
お年より	おとしより	aged people
回	かい	times
気持ちがいい	きもちがいい	to feel good
今日	きょう	today
高校	こうこう	high school
高校生	こうこうせい	high school student
今年	ことし	this year
子どもの時	こどものとき	when I was a child
今晩	こんばん	tonight
しあいに出る	しあいにでる	to participate in a match
時間	じかん	time
時間わり	じかんわり	timetable
自転車	じてんしゃ	bicycle
下手な	へたな	bad at/unskillful
新聞部	しんぶんぶ	newspaper club
生活	せいかつ	life/lifestyle
せが高い	せがたかい	tall
父	ちち	father *(your own)*
電話	でんわ	telephone
東京	とうきょう	Tokyo
土俵	どひょう	sumo ring
ながい間	ながいあいだ	for a long time
名前	なまえ	name
何才	なんさい	how old?
年齢	ねんれい	age
母	はは	mother *(your own)*
入っている	はいっている	to belong to
人々	ひとびと	people
二日毎に	ふつかごとに	every other day
町	まち	city/town
見つける	みつける	to find
物	もの	things

Unit 3

あさごはん	breakfast
あびる	to bathe
あらう	to wash/clean
アルバイト	part-time job
うるさい	noisy
うわばき	indoor shoes
おんすいプール	heated swimming pool
かける	to wear *(glasses)*
かつ	to win
かどうぶ	ikebana/flower arranging club
かぶる	to wear *(hat)*
かみのけ	hair
かむ	to chew
かれ	he
かんたんな	easy
きじ	article
きそく	rules
きちんと	neatly/properly
きょうしつ	classroom
(お)けしょう(する)	make-up *(to wear make-up)*
けいざい	economics
げた	clogs
げたばこ	shoe locker
けど	but *(casual speech)*
さいごに	finally
さがす	to search/look for
さくぶん	essay
さどうぶ	tea ceremony club
じゅぎょう	class/lesson
じゅんびたいそう	warm-up exercises
すう	to smoke
せいふく	uniform
そうじ（する）	cleaning *(to clean)*
たいいくさい	sports festival
たいそう	gymnastics
たつ	to stand
たとえば	for example
たばこ	tobacco/cigarettes
ちがう	to differ
ちこく（する）	lateness *(to be late)*
つかれる	to get tired
つく	to arrive
つける	to wear *(accessories, jewellery)*
でんとうてきな	traditional
ぬぐ	to take off *(clothes, shoes)*
はく	to wear *(lower half)*
はじまる	*(something)* starts
バッジ	badge
びじゅつ	art
ふうせんガム	bubble gum
ぶかつ	school club(s)
ぶんぼうぐや	stationery shop

(お) へんじ	reply
ほうかご	after school
まず	first of all
みじかい	short
めずらしい	unusual/rare
もつ	to have/hold
もらう	to receive
ようふく	clothes
りくじょうぶ	athletics club
れい	a bow
ろうか	corridor
わかい	young

先	さき、せん	future, previous
生	う(まれる)、い(きる)、なま、しょう、せい	to be born
学	まな(ぶ)、がく	to learn
校	こう	school
家	いえ、うち、や、か	house, home
自	じ	self, in person
出	で(る)、で(かける)、だ(す)、しゅつ	to leave, to go out
入	いり、い(れる)、はい(る)、にゅう	to enter, to put in

会う	あう	to meet
言う	いう	to say/tell
一時間目	いちじかんめ	period one
一日中	いちにちじゅう	all day/throughout the day
学期	がっき	school term
去年	きょねん	last year
携帯電話	けいたいでんわ	mobile phone
校舎	こうしゃ	school building
校則	こうそく	school rules
国語	こくご	Japanese language *(national language)*
今度	こんど	next time
自分の	じぶんの	my/your own
先週	せんしゅう	last week
大学	だいがく	university
中	ちゅう/じゅう	during
手紙	てがみ	letter
出る	でる	to leave/depart
時々	ときどき	sometimes
(の)時に	(の)ときに	when/at the time of
人気	にんき	popularity
入る	はいる	to enter/go in
はじめての日	はじめてのひ	first day
分かる	わかる	to understand
私たち	わたしたち	we

Unit 4

(あるき) はじめる	to begin to *(walk)*
あんしんする	to be relieved
いけ	lake
いし	stone
いたい	it hurts!
いと	thread
いのる	to pray
いっぱい (な)	full
うそをつく	to tell lies
うんてんする	to drive
Eメール	e-mail
おい!	Hey!
おおぜいの	many
おくってくれませんか	would you send me?
おしえてあげます	I will teach you
おちる	to fall down
おてら	Buddhist temple
おひるになる	to become noon
おぼうさん	Buddhist priest
おぼえる	to remember
おりる	to get down
おりろ!	Get down!
おれ	I/me *(male speech)*
おろす	to lower down
おわり	The end
おわる	to finish
かお	face
かっこいい	cool
かなしい	sad
かわいそう	such a pity
かんぬし	Shinto priest
きれる	to cut off
きょうみぶかい	very interesting
くも	spider
けっこん (する)	marriage *(to get married)*
けんか	fight
ごくらく	heaven
こまのようにくるくるとまわって	spinning like a top
ころす	to kill
サウスパーク	South Park *(cartoon)*
さる	monkey
じごく	hell
(お) しゃかさま	Buddha
しゅうきょう	religion
しゅぎょうする	to practise the simple life
しょうひん	product
ジョギング	jogging
しれん	trials
しんとう	Shinto
すぐ	soon
そうだなあ	well, let me see *(male speech)*

そら	sky
たすける	to help
ダンス	dance
ちず	map
ちょうど	just
つかう	to use
つける	to put on
つづける	to continue
つりがね	hanging bell
とう	pagoda
とつぜん	suddenly
とまる	to stop
とりい	*torii* gate
ならう	to learn
なりたい	want to become
ぬすむ	to steal
のせる	to put on/to place on
のぼると	if I climb
はじめる	*(I)* start
はな	flowers
はり	needles
フィクション	fiction
ぶっきょう	Buddhism
ぶっきょうと	Buddhist
ぶつぞう	statue of Buddha
ピアノ	piano
ペーパーバック	paperback
ほかの	other
ほそい	thin
まもる	to protect
やっと	finally
ゆっくりと	slowly
ようこそ	welcome
ロマンス	romance

雨がふる	あめがふる	it will rain *(it rains)*
生きている時	いきているとき	when *(he)* was alive
行こう	いこう	let's go
一日に	いちにちに	in one day
先	さき	ahead
木	き	tree
神社	じんじゃ	Shinto shrine
水泳	すいえい	swimming
先月	せんげつ	last month
その時	そのとき	at that time
小さく見える	ちいさくみえる	to appear small
ながい間	ながいあいだ	for a long time
日記	にっき	diary
人たち	ひとたち	people

ひる休み	ひるやすみ	lunchtime break
火をつける	ひをつける	to light a fire
見つける	みつける	to find
もって行く	もっていく	to take something
物語	ものがたり	tale
旅行する	りょこうする	to travel

Unit 5

あかるいせいかく	cheerful personality
アドベンチャーランド	Adventure Land
いいけいけんになる	to be a good experience
いそがしい	busy
いっしょうけんめい	try as hard as you can
いる	to need/to exist/to be
いやな	unpleaseant/disgusting
ウエイトレス	waitress
うんてんめんきょ	driver's licence
おきゃくさん	customer
おそく	late
おもちゃ	toy
ガイド	guide
ガイドブック	guide book
かえる	to return home
カヌー	canoe
かばん	bag
カメラマン	camera operator/photographer
かよいはじめました	I started to attend
かよう	to attend *(school)*
(〜に) かよっている	I attend
かんこう	sightseeing
かんこうガイド	tour guide
かんこうち	sightseeing spots
キックボクシング	kick boxing
きめる	to decide
きゅうじんこうこく	job advertisement
きょうし	teacher
くつ	shoes
クッキー	cookies
くまのプーさん	Winnie the Pooh
クレジットカード	credit card
コーチ	coach
こたえる	to answer
コンピュータープログラマー	computer programmer
さくぶん	essay
サングラス	sunglasses
CDプレーヤー	CD player
しごと	job
Gショック	"G Shock"
シスタースクール	sister school

しつもん	questions
しつれいします	Goodbye *(often used to end a telephone call)*
しょうかいする	to introduce
じょうぶな	sturdy
ジャングルクルーズ	Jungle Cruise
シャンプー	shampoo
しゅみ	hobbies
ジーンズ	jeans
スターツアーズ	Star Tours
スーツ	suit
ずっと	all the time
スニカー	sneakers
スペースマウンテン	Space Mountain
スモールワールド	It's a small world
せいせき	*(school)* report/results
せいせきひょう	report card
せつめい（する）	explanation *(to explain)*
そうぞうりょく	creativity
タオル	towel
ちかい	near
Tシャツ	T-shirt
てんいん	shop assistant
とくに	especially
ドーナツ	doughnut
ドナルドダック	Donald Duck
ドライヤー	hair dryer
ならう	to learn
はさみ	scissors
パスポート	passport
はじめての	first
はずかしい	embarrassed
はたらく	to work
(〜で) はたらいている	I'm working/I work at
パーティードレス	party dress
パレード	parade
ビッグサンダーマウンテン	Big Thunder Mountain
ビーチバレーボール	beach volleyball
びょういん	hospital
ブティック	boutique
プロゴルファー	professional golfer
ヘアクリップ	hair clip
ほうそう	broadcast
(〜が) ほしいです	I want
ポータブルCDプレーヤー	portable CD player
マウスパッド	mouse pad
マネージャー	manager
マグカップ	mug
まど	window
ミッキーマウス	Mickey Mouse
ミニーマウス	Minnie Mouse
むすめ	daughter *(your own)*
むすこ	son *(your own)*
めんきょ	licence
めんせつ	interview *(job)*
もうすこし	a little more
もちろん	of course
モデルクラブ	modelling club
やめる	to quit
ヨーロッパ	Europe
ライオンキング	Lion King
ラジオ	radio
りょうり	cooking/dish
レポート	report
わすれる	to forget

母	はは、かあ	mother
父	ちち、とう	father
英	えい	England
語	ご	word
話	はな（す）、わ	to speak
書	か（く）、しょ	to write
来	く（る）、らい	to come
会	あ（う）、かい	to meet

英会話	えいかいわ	English conversation
お母さん	おかあさん	mother
お金	おかね	money
思う	おもう	to think
外国語	がいこくご	foreign language
会社	かいしゃ	company
会社員	かいしゃいん	office/company employee
家庭教師	かていきょうし	home tutor
書き方	かきかた	how to write
聞く	きく	listen/ask
きょうみがある人	きょうみがあるひと	interested people
子犬	こいぬ	puppy
子猫	こねこ	kitten
時給	じきゅう	hourly wages
自己紹介	じこしょうかい	self-introduction
辞書	じしょ	dictionary
出す	だす	to submit/put out
食べ物	たべもの	food
誕生日	たんじょうび	birthday
電子辞書	でんしじしょ	electronic dictionary
電話番号	でんわばんごう	telephone number
動物	どうぶつ	animal
動物園	どうぶつえん	zoo
飲み物	のみもの	beverage
飲む	のむ	to drink

病気	びょうき	ill/sick
貿易会社	ぼうえきがいしゃ	trading company
水着	みずぎ	swimsuit/bathers
名刺	めいし	business card
旅行	りょこう	travelling
旅行会社	りょこうがいしゃ	travel agency
留学する	りゅうがくする	to study abroad
履歴書	りれきしょ	curriculum vitae/resume

Unit 6

あんないする	to guide
いなか	the country
うたう	to sing
うんがいい	to have good luck
おちゃや	tea house
おどり	*(traditional)* dance
おどる	to dance
おみやげ	souvenir
おみやげや	souvenir shop
おりる	to get off/get down from
かかる	to take time
かど	corner
がわ	side
かんこうきゃく	tourist
キロメートル	kilometres
くうこう	airport
げきじょう	theatre
こうさてん	intersection
コンビニ	convenience store
しゅと	capital city
しょくいんしつ	staff room
しんごう	traffic lights
すごす	to spend time
せまい	narrow
そうすると	and then
そこ	there
つきあたり	T-intersection
〜と	when/if
どうやって	how
とおる	to pass/go along
どちら	where
のりかえる	to change *(transport)*
のりば	platform
のる	to get onto/to ride
はし	bridge
バスてい	bus stop
びじゅつかん	art gallery
ぶんか	culture
へん	area/vicinity
(〜の) ほう	in the direction of
まがる	to turn
まっすぐ	straight
まよう	to get lost
みせ	shop
みち	road/street
(〜て) みる	to try *(doing)*
むかし	long ago
ゆうがた	evening
りょかん	traditional Japanese inn
わたる	to cross

北	きた、ほく	north
南	みなみ、なん	south
東	ひがし、とう	east
西	にし、せい	west
町	まち、ちょう	town
物	もの、ぶつ	thing
食	た (べる)、しょく	to eat
飲	の (む)	to drink

一日目	いちにちめ	the first day
今から	いまから	from now on
運転手さん	うんてんしゅさん	driver
お父さん	おとうさん	father
外国人	がいこくじん	foreigner
改札口	かいさつぐち	ticket gate
外食 (する)	がいしょく (する)	eating out *(to eat out)*
北	きた	north
見物する	けんぶつする	to go sightseeing
午前中	ごぜんちゅう	during the morning
修学旅行	しゅうがくりょこう	school trip
自由行動	じゆうこうどう	free activities
新幹線	しんかんせん	bullet train
外	そと	outside
地下鉄	ちかてつ	subway
中心	ちゅうしん	centre
図書館	としょかん	library
西	にし	west
日程	にってい	itinerary
博物館	はくぶつかん	museum
東	ひがし	east
東口	ひがしぐち	east exit
飛行機	ひこうき	aeroplane
左	ひだり	left
左がわ	ひだりがわ	left side
舞子さん	まいこさん	traditional dancing girls in Kyoto
右	みぎ	right
南	みなみ	south

Places

熱海	あたみ	Atami
上野(動物園)	うえの（どうぶつえん）	Ueno *(zoo)*
大阪	おおさか	Osaka
金沢	かなざわ	Kanazawa
祇園	ぎおん	Gion
九州	きゅうしゅう	Kyushu
京都	きょうと	Kyoto
清水寺	きよみずでら	Kiyomizu Temple
金閣寺	きんかくじ	Kinkaku Temple
銀座	ぎんざ	Ginza
熊本	くまもと	Kumamoto
神戸	こうべ	Kobe
札幌	さっぽろ	Sapporo
三条京阪	さんじょうけいはん	Sanjo-Keihan
四国	しこく	Shikoku
四条	しじょう	Shijo
静岡	しずおか	Shizuoka
品川	しながわ	Shinagawa
渋谷	しぶや	Shibuya
新宿	しんじゅく	Shinjuku
仙台	せんだい	Sendai
東京	とうきょう	Tokyo
長崎	ながさき	Nagasaki
奈良	なら	Nara
新潟	にいがた	Niigata
二条城	にじょうじょう	Nijo Castle
日光	にっこう	Nikko
函館	はこだて	Hakodate
箱根	はこね	Hakone
姫路	ひめじ	Himeji
広島	ひろしま	Hiroshima
富士山	ふじさん	Mt Fuji
北海道	ほっかいどう	Hokkaido
本州	ほんしゅう	Honshu
松山	まつやま	Matsuyama
山形県	やまがたけん	Yamagata Prefecture
竜安寺	りょうあんじ	Ryoan Temple

Unit 7

43130

あかちゃん	baby
あきかん	empty can
あきびん	empty bottle
あげる	*(I)* give
あてる	to shine on
いす	chair
いなくなった	disappeared *(people)*
ウール	wool
うら	back/underside
オイル	oil
えいきょう	influence
おおい	many/lots
おきる	to get up
おす	to push
おそくまで	until late
おもて	front/topside
おんだんか	global warming
かえる	to change
かじょうほうそう	excess wrapping
かならず	without fail
かみ	paper
かん	can
かんがえる	to think
かんきょうもんだい	environmental problems
きちょうな	precious/valuable
けす	to turn off/switch off
ごみ	rubbish
ごみおきば	rubbish disposal area
ごみばこ	rubbish bin
コンクール	competition
さわる	to touch
じょうほう	information
しらべる	to look up/research
すてる	to throw out
すべりだい	slide *(playground)*
せかい	world
せっけん	soap
せつやく（する）	conservation *(to conserve)*
だけ	only
ためす	to attempt
だんだん	gradually
ちきゅう	earth
ちきゅうおんだんか	global warming of the Earth
ちきゅうにやさしく	be kind to the Earth
ちゅうもんする	to order
つきあう	to date
テーマ	theme
できている	to be made of
～てみよう	let's try
どこでも	everywhere
どこにも	nowhere
とめる	to stop
なくなる	to disappear *(things)*
にる	to be similar to
ねんりょう	fuel
はをみがく	to brush one's teeth
バケツ	bucket
ばしょ	place
ひかり	light *(beam)*
びっくりする	to be surprised

ビニールぶくろ	plastic bag
ひろう	to pick up
びん	bottle
ふく	clothing
ふくろ	bag
プラスチック	plastic
ぶんぼうぐ	equipment/stationery
ペットボトル	recyclable plastic bottle
べつべつ（に）	separately
へる	to decrease
ホース	hose
ほご（する）	protection *(to protect)*
まとめる	to tie up
まもる	to protect
まわる	to go around
みがく	to polish/brush
めんどうくさい	annoying/troublesome
もえないごみ	non-burnable waste
もえるごみ	burnable waste
もったいない	wasteful
もっと	more
もどす	to restore/turn back
もとにもどす	to return to original state
もんだい	problem/issue
やめる	to give up
ゆめ	dream
ゆめのしま	Dream Island
よくなった	*(have)* become better
リサイクル（する）	recycling *(to recycle)*
リサイクルよう	for the purpose of recycling
れいぞうこ	fridge
わりばし	disposable chopsticks

川	かわ	river
海	うみ、かい	sea
国	くに、こく	country
外	そと、がい	outside
友	とも、ゆう	friend
社	しゃ	company
思	おも（う）	to think
言	い(う)、こと、げん	to say

一歩ずつ	いっぽずつ	step by step
外国	がいこく	foreign country
会社	かいしゃ	company
科学者	かがくしゃ	scientist
川	かわ	river
金属	きんぞく	metal
国	くに	country
国立公園	こくりつこうえん	National Park
小道	こみち	small street
自然	しぜん	nature

社会	しゃかい	society
食器洗い	しょっきあらい	dishwasher
植物	しょくぶつ	plants
数学	すうがく	mathematics
大変な	たいへんな	grave/serious/terrible/difficult
大切な	たいせつな	important/valuable
大事な	だいじな	serious/importnat
食べ物をやる	たべものをやる	to give *(animals)* food
電気製品	でんきせいひん	electrical goods
電池	でんち	battery
生ごみ	なまごみ	food waste
何でも	なんでも	anything
何でもない	なんでもない	nothing
二か月	にかげつ	two months
一晩中	ひとばんじゅう	all night
病気になる	びょうきになる	to become sick
本当	ほんとう	really
毎朝	まいあさ	every morning
学ぶ	まなぶ	to learn
野性動物	やせいどうぶつ	wild animals
分ける	わける	to divide/separate

Unit 8

あちこち	here and there
あぶない	dangerous
いいこと	good points
いらしてください	please come
オーディション	audition
おく	to put
おさら	plate/dish
おせんされた	has become polluted
おなかがすく	to be hungry
うわあい！	Yeah!
かいけつ（する）	solution *(to solve)*
かいだん	steps/stairs
かいとうしゃ	panel
(が) ほしい時に	when you want
(と) くらべると	if you compare it to
けいけん（する）	experience *(to experience)*
このあたり	around here
これから	from now on
さあ、行こう！	Come on/let's go!
さて	well/now *(to change the subject)*
さま	Ms/Mr *(very formal)*
ざぶとん	cushion
すいている	I am hungry
ぜひ	by all means

センチ	centimetres
そうだんする	to consult
～そうです	I hear you did
ソブリン・ヒル	Sovereign Hill *(place)*
たいけん（する）	experience *(to experience)*
たつ	to build
たび	journey
チワワ	Chihuahua
つつ	tube
テレビばんぐみ	television programme
てん	points
とくてん	scores
ところ	place
どこに行くのだろう	I wonder where it goes?
とる	to receive *(a medal)*/to take
ながれる	to flow
なげる	to throw
なやみ	a worry/a problem
なやみそうだんしつ	advice corner
はつめい	invention
はつめいじっけんしつ	invention laboratory
はつめいしゃ	inventor
バララット	Ballarat *(place)*
バレーボール	volleyball
ビクトリアしゅう	*(State of)* Victoria
フィリップとう	Phillip Island
ふとん	Japanese style bedding
ペンキン・パレード	Penguin Parade
もうちきゅうのどこにも行くところはありません。	There's nowhere else to go on Earth.
やったー！	Yeah!
よぶ	to call
ゆび	finger
りゆう	reason
りょうしん	parents
わらう	to laugh
わるいこと	bad points

雨水	あまみず	rainwater
雨がふったら	あめがふったら	if it rains
雨の時	あめのとき	when it rains
大人	おとな	adults
海岸	かいがん	beach
金鉱	きんこう	gold mine
銀行	ぎんこう	bank
司会者	しかいしゃ	compere
自己紹介する	じこしょうかいする	to give a self-introduction
自動的に	じどうてきに	automatically
新宿駅	しんじゅくえき	Shinjuku station
水上スキー	すいじょうスキー	water skiing
第一部	だいいちぶ	first part
太陽電池	たいようでんち	solar battery
～段	だん	steps *(counter for steps, stairs)*
出る	でる	to attend/take part in
何をしているかしら？	なにをしているかしら？	I wonder what they are doing?
二段ベッド	にだんベッド	bunk bed
昼の間に	ひるのあいだに	during the day
見つかる	みつかる	to be found/sighted
見るのは	みるのは	the ones you see
もんくを言わないで！	もんくをいわないで！	Stop complaining!